FOOTNOTES

Praise for *Footnotes*:

"Cameron Anstee's *Footnotes* is a love letter to the bookshelf; how Canadian publishers have created strange and wonderous titles which occupy our desks, thoughts, and dreams. Like a walk down a wooded trail with the finest of park rangers, Anstee points at the titles and presses which sprout, like mushrooms and wildflowers, along the path. I adore this book and the thoughtful, generous conversations that Anstee has brought to our homes."

—DEREK BEAULIEU,
author of *Do It Wrong: How to be a Poet in the 21st Century*

"Don't let the title deceive you: these fascinating, meticulous essays are much more than footnotes. Anstee skillfully unspools the stories behind a handful of under-the-radar small press publishers and projects to showcase a breadth of Canadian talent past and present. A love letter to ink, long-arm staplers, and artistic potential, *Footnotes* is an essential catalogue of small press publishing and inspiration for would-be bookmakers."

—LEIGH NASH, publisher of Assembly Press

"If you are a poet, a small- or micro-press publisher, or a writer of experimental non/fiction, if you are enthralled by works of innovation and daring, if you have a passion for imaginative reading experiences that celebrate the overlooked and the radical, then Cameron Anstee's *Footnotes* is for you. These essays will leave you, in Robert Bringhurst's words, 'eager to encounter the originals', of which Anstee writes so captivatingly."

—BETH FOLLETT, author of *Instructor*

FOOTNOTES:

Case Studies in Canadian Small Press Bookmaking

CAMERON ANSTEE

Copyright © Cameron Anstee 2026
All rights reserved

Palimpsest Press
1171 Eastlawn Ave.
Windsor, Ontario. N8S 3J1
www.palimpsestpress.ca

Printed and bound in Canada
Cover design and typesetting by Ellie Hastings
Edited by Jim Johnstone
Cover photograph by Jennifer Huzera

Palimpsest Press would like to thank the Canada Council for the Arts and the Ontario Arts Council for their support of our publishing program. We also acknowledge the assistance of the Government of Ontario through the Ontario Book Publishing Tax Credit.

LIBRARY AND ARCHIVES CANADA CATALOGUING IN PUBLICATION

TITLE: Footnotes : case studies in Canadian small press bookmaking / Cameron Anstee.
NAMES: Anstee, Cameron, author.
IDENTIFIERS: Canadiana (print) 20260237221
Canadiana (ebook) 20260239984
ISBN 9781997508212 (SOFTCOVER) | ISBN 9781997508229 (EPUB)
SUBJECTS: LCSH: Small presses—Canada.

CLASSIFICATION: LCC Z231.5.L5 A57 2026 | DDC 070.50971—DC23

For my father, Rod Anstee, and our joint holdings
For my partner, Jenn, and our life full of books

Contents

Introduction

> "To say it seems simplistic, but I will give it a try—there are all different kinds of books of poetry. That's it, there are all different kinds of books of poetry. Not that there are all different kinds of poetry that end up in books, which I think of as the more common sense of it. But that unlike most other forms of writing, poetry shoves, nudges, and creates its own spaces. And the only way to really express this, and the only way I imagine to express that cosmos of formal possibility, would be to describe hundreds of books, hundreds and hundreds of books. Not their poems, exactly, but their forms and the forms they came to have because of their poetry."
>
> —Joshua Beckman, *Three Talks* (2018)

Without understanding that it was happening, I received an education in mid- and late-twentieth century book design during my childhood. My father, Rod Anstee, had what was likely the largest collection of Kerouac and Beat literature in Canada at the time. Ours was a house full of books and as people who live in such houses know, that meant an ongoing process of sorting, shelving, culling, re-sorting, and re-shelving to wrestle a perpetually precarious order. I can see now what a privilege it was to grow up in such an environment, one in which books—remarkable books—were simply a daily presence. The collection was of such scale and significance that I remember visits from people my father had become acquainted with through its assembly, among them Carolyn Cassidy, Jim Christy, and George Bowering. And so I shelved and re-shelved in service to that collection, and eventually I started reading once I realized what I had been handling, all the while absorbing what I can now see were formative influences for my own tastes in book design—Grove Press's combination of abstract expressionist art with inspired typographic design; the evocative bursts of colour on the Viking first editions of Kerouac's *On the Road* and *The Dharma Bums*; the distinctive black and white photographs blazoned on covers from New Directions; the spare, expressive typography of the City Lights Pocket Poets series; the strikingly diminutive scale of Hanuman Books; and the scores of weirder smaller books from weirder smaller presses that my father continues to be adept at finding.

The book in your hands documents, in part, how I learned to look at and handle books—and to a lesser degree, how to make them—in the decades that have elapsed since, something I began to do in a concerted way during my undergraduate studies. I worked as an editor at Collett Tracey's In/Words Magazine and Press while completing my B.A. in English Literature at Carleton University in Ottawa in the mid-2000s, an experience which taught me the basics of making chapbooks while instilling my first understanding of how many people in this corner of the world were producing exceptionally interesting and well-made books. That is to say, it taught me how little I knew, how much better so many others seemed to be at the thing I wanted to do, and how to seek out ways to learn. I have a vivid memory of a lecture Collett gave about Contact Press during my second-year

Canadian literature survey; I can see the room and where I was sitting, and I can hear her reading a letter that Louis Dudek wrote to Raymond Souster and Irving Layton in 1952 when they were weighing whether or not to found the press:

> Yes, goddamit, let's get ourselves out a book of our own, the three of us, and piss on the presses. The poet has to publish his own work henceforth, if he wants to print more than 12 pages in SIX YEARS ... The whole system stinks, when 1000000000 advertisements get mass distribution and a few poems get 250 copies on toilet paper.

To this day that letter reverberates in my head when I think of the impact of the small press (even as I feel, more and more strongly each year, that 12 pages every six years in editions of 250 copies would suit me beautifully as a rate of production). It is the spirit of it that stays with me, the impulse to figure out how to publish with the tools at hand in a way that suits the work.

In classrooms, libraries, and bookstores, and at small press book fairs and poetry readings, I began to learn about the Canadian small press, past and present. In the stacks at the MacOdrum Library, I handled and admired books from Contact, Coach House, Weed/Flower, and other legendary presses of the 1960s and 1970s, books I mostly could not afford unless I lucked into finding beat-up copies at cheap prices. Like anyone who starts hanging around in small press communities, I then quickly encountered the long-serving and seemingly tireless Proper Tales Press, CURVD H&z, and above/ground press, each with a clear identity and distinctive design aesthetic, and each offering a different model for contributing and committing to the small press. Moreover, at the Ottawa Small Press Book Fair, I found chapbook makers who were more or less my age but were somehow already doing astonishing and imaginative work, among them The

Emergency Response Unit, Ferno House, and Puddles of Sky. To my amazement and delight, I learned that I could afford (or trade for) their books! And all the while, in those formative years, my partner and I wandered in bookstores and art galleries, broadening my awareness of what was happening, what had happened, and what was possible.

Book design became a formal component of my research life in the next decade during my doctoral studies, which were focused primarily on small press bookselling. A handful of the essays here were first given in early forms as conference papers that served as outlets for my thinking. They also evolved in parallel with my own development as a maker of books through my chapbook press, Apt. 9 Press, and the growth of my personal small press library. With limited resources, I aspire to make and collect good books, and as I hope *Footnotes* shows, I embrace a fairly broad conception of what a good book is—that is, a well-written, well-designed, and well-made book.

The central argument of these essays is simple—if one cares about books and about the small press and wants to understand each as fully as possible, one should look at how books are constructed as objects and as ideas, at the breadth of how the small press conceives of what a book might be, and at how readers are asked to engage with small press books of various sorts. I will not refer to this as even a modest insight—indeed the argument has been made by many thinkers in many places, small press or otherwise, over many years and is a foundational concept in studies of print culture. D.F. McKenzie, for example, in his seminal 1986 book *Bibliography and the Sociology of Texts*, argues that bibliography is "the only discipline which has consistently studied the composition, formal design, and transmission of texts by writers, printers, and publishers; their distribution through different communities by wholesalers, retailers, and teachers; their collection and classification by librarians, their meaning for, and—I must add—their creative regenerations by readers."

What I try to do in these pages is put this idea to work by focusing on Canadian small press bookmakers who have received, in my opinion, inadequate attention for their labour.

It is, of course, necessary to define my terms, but attempting to define the "small press" means confronting a vast and varied body of work in a staggering range of forms. I've tried to put forward concise definitions of the small press in various places over the years with varying degrees of success. Recently, I tried it more or less in this way:[1] small press activities in Canada today encompass a range of different types of productions, from trade presses with national and international footprints to chapbook and micropresses that operate on a smaller scale; from perfect-bound, nationally distributed objects to handmade, photocopied efforts that circulate in hyper-local networks; from free handouts, to public performances, to websites, to blogs, to still other types of publications. Whether defined broadly as a form of independent publishing, a rhizomatic "network of multiple, asymmetrical, interconnected nodes" (Butling and Rudy), an "amorphous totality" (beaulieu and Christie), or a form of opposition to the "prevailing discourses of modern society" (Jones), the small press is constituted in part by the intimate relationship that it posits between writing, publishing, and reading. Writers who publish with small presses are, more often than not, also small press editors, publishers, book designers, organizers of public events, critics, and primary readers. Two decades into the twenty-first century, the small press remains proudly resistant to concise definition. I hope that the essays contained in this book will illuminate some portion of the vitality, energy, oppositional spirit, and highly personal components of the small press—and of small press bookmaking—that render it so elusive and defiant.

---

1 This attempted definition is based on one provided in my contribution to the collection *Unpacking the Personal Library: The Public and Private Life of Books* (Waterloo: Wilfrid Laurier University Press, 2022), edited by Jason Camlot and J.A. Weingarten.

Footnotes is arranged as a series of case studies in small press bookmaking—not an exhaustive historical overview. Common concerns animate these essays, but they are open-ended starting points. The first essay looks at the work of Fran Jones and Robert Rosewarne, leaders of a small-but-mighty small press community in Ottawa in the early 1960s that was firmly at odds with Ottawa's reputation as a government town. The character of their work is intimately connected to it having been produced in the Capital, but this fact also rendered it largely absent from the greater small press literary record in Canada. The second essay examines the work of visual artist Barbara Caruso as a publisher and writer of experimental poetry in the 1970s and 1980s. Caruso's publishing relied primarily on serigraph and rubberstamp, and was notably sensitive to the scale of her books—an awareness derived from her life as a visual artist—rendering her publications difficult, if not impossible, to reproduce effectively. The third essay examines the design work of Eva Fritsch on the first edition of Robert Kroetsch's *Seed Catalogue* (1977), tracing her contributions as a collaborator to the meaning(s) of the poem and book to recuperate the print history of one of the most studied poems in Canadian literature. The fourth essay considers two "fetish objects" created by Christine McNair to celebrate significant anniversaries of rob mclennan's above/ground press in the 2010s, arguing that McNair deftly negotiates her role as designer to balance the principles of fine press and the particular material and design histories of above/ground press. The fifth essay looks at the print manifestation of a primarily non-print project from Jessica Bebenek—*k2tog* (2018), a Risograph-printed book of knitting patterns and photographs that offers a feminist engagement with a specific set of poems by women and interdisciplinary modes of public performance and dissemination. Finally, the sixth essay thinks through Justin Million's KEYBOARDS! project, a massive 500-poem undertaking completed in 2018 that was both a print expression of poetry (via typewriter) and a live performance that actively resisted the idea of *the book* while embracing a gift economic mode of distribution.

While some of the work discussed in these pages adheres to traditional concepts of excellence in book design and production, some of it discards them. Despite many authoritative books on the principles of book design insisting that content and design must work effectively together, the examples of excellence commonly cited have certain similarities in design regardless of content. There are variations—in typeface, page dimensions, and materials, to say nothing of the exceptional variety of typographic design itself—but it is rare to encounter non-traditional or small press books and objects in these studies. Indeed, it is most often the private press that is central in such discussions, a term that denotes letterpress and largely excludes the kinds of small press work discussed here. Some of the designers and bookmakers examined in this book do use letterpress, but they also use linocut, rubberstamp, serigraph, photocopy, typewriter, and Risograph to produce their works. This variety reflects the tools and resources at their disposal. Their output includes lyric poems, concrete poems, and poems translated into knitting patterns. They published books, anthologies, broadsides, and other stranger objects that are more difficult to classify. Some of the books received traditional trade distribution, while others hewed to the extreme end of a restricted gift economy.

David McKnight, writing in *History of the Book in Canada: Volume Three: 1918–1980* (2007), identifies the "consultative relationship that often exists between publisher and author in determining layout and appearance" as the distinguishing feature of how small presses approach book design, and makes the point that "[w]hile aesthetics and craft feature in the production and physical appearance of little magazines and small press titles [...] economic concerns exert ongoing influence." His point is two-fold—small press publishers must "perform a variety of functions, including editing, design, and production" to operate within limited economic means, and that many "employ inexpensive office print technologies" for production. While such conditions can have the effect of limiting what is possible for a small press in terms of design and production, they also provide a tremendous amount of freedom. The creativity that is necessitated by limited economic means, as well as the freedom from other kinds of constraints it can offer (such as from the expectations of the book trade), allow these presses to produce exciting, innovative, and unique books.

It would be inaccurate to suggest that small press books are never recognized or celebrated for their design. A brief albeit incomplete overview of significant venues and publications makes clear that there are critics and other small press folks paying attention. Robert Bringhurst's landmark *The Surface of Meaning: Books and Book Design in Canada* (2008) focuses in part on "the visual and sculptural coming-of-age of the Canadian printed book." Bringhurst is attentive to many different kinds of presses, from trade and university presses to small and fine presses, and so in *The Surface of Meaning* the reader finds the University of Toronto Press and McClelland & Stewart beside Periwinkle Press and blewointment, as well as a remarkable discussion of "Canada's wealth of Aboriginal traditions, in which the books are still primarily oral."[2] David McKnight's recent and lavishly illustrated *Experiment: Printing the Canadian Imagination* (2018), the published catalogue to an exhibition of his small press collection, makes clear McKnight's love of the small press as well as his delight in the shapes and forms small press books may take. Jim Johnstone's *Write, Print, Fold and Staple:*

2 Bringhurst also offers the following definition of "one kind of press that seems to [him] distinctly Canadian": "It is easily described as a hybrid between the literary trade press and the private press, but it was not in fact created by cross-breeding. It is typically modest in size but has national distribution, and it is run like a Renaissance publishing house, printing what it publishes and devoting as much attention to physical workmanship as to literary values." Bringhurst dates the birth of this Canadian form of the small trade press to Stan Bevington and Coach House in 1965, and cites The Porcupine's Quill and Gaspereau Press as "current leading examples."

On Poetry and Micropress in Canada (Gaspereau Press, 2023) is a celebration of the humble "small and provisional" presses that operate "outside of the commercial anxieties of trade publishing, pursuing unmediated aesthetic, cultural and personal aims." I think, too, of *DA: A Journal of the Printing Arts* (previously *The Devil's Artisan*), which showed an admirable eagerness to examine the more radical publishing experiments in Canada's literary history but which sadly ceased publication as of issue 93 (Fall/Winter 2023), of the late *Open Letter*, which consistently created space to look closely at all facets of the small press, of the Alcuin Society and their journal *Amphora*, of the Bibliographical Society of Canada, and of remarkable catalogues from Canada's past and present booksellers who are deeply invested in the small press.

Yet, despite all of that, I feel that the small press is still in some way hard done by, that the variety in small press approaches to making books often seems to be missing from broader studies of book history and book design in Canada. Justified or not, that feeling is responsible for the impulse to write these essays, and to pry open the field in other ways. My work is primarily attuned to activities outside of the dominant centre of small press publishing in Canada—that is, outside of Toronto—looking instead at Ottawa, Paris (Ontario), Winnipeg, Montreal, and Peterborough. Perhaps most significantly, *Footnotes* primarily (but not exclusively) examines the work of female bookmakers and designers. The history of book and typographic design in Canada is often focused on a small number of exceptional male artists—Frank Newfeld, Glenn Goluska, Carl Dair, Leslie Smart, Allan Fleming, Robert Reid, Takao Tanabe, and Jim Rimmer, to cite some of the most common names. Antje Lingner, in-house book designer at the University of Toronto Press for four decades starting in the mid-1950s, is one woman likely to appear in such lists. Artist Betty Sutherland's design work with mid-century small presses First Statement and Contact is another notable exception.

These elements open to a larger set of questions. While my title declares these to be case studies in small press book*making*, they could be reasonably categorized under small press book *history*. I approach the field of book history with a broad lens that encompasses literary history, textual analysis, and bibliography. My own interest and emphasis fall most heavily, perhaps, on bibliography, but based on an expansive understanding of the term as per McKenzie, who wrote that, "Bibliography is the discipline that studies texts as recorded forms, and the processes of their transmission, including their reproduction and reception." Throughout, I use book history as an umbrella to think about how book design, print history, and bibliography are intertwined. My initial focus on bookmaking is a jumping-off point to look at issues related to modes of production, aesthetic content, and the particular goals of a writer or publisher. These issues lead to a consideration of reception, collection, and preservation. What does it look like, in the small press, for book design to serve content? How do design choices affect reproduction, and whether work is (or even can be) anthologized? How does production affect how works are preserved and accessed by future generations? How can the study of bookmaking be calibrated to issues specific to the small press?

Footnotes is also an opportunity to satisfy my love of bibliographic digression. The most indulgent component of this book is the inclusion of detailed historical and bibliographical information. I love bibliography—I love the things that can be learned about books and about culture from it and from the range of other paratextual materials to be found in or near books. Paratexts, from Gerard Genette, are "devices and conventions [...] that mediate the book to the reader." These devices—which can include seemingly simple elements internal to a book, such as titles, prefaces, and dedications, as well as more complex public elements that dwell outside of the book, such as interviews, reviews, and public performances—"surround" and "extend" a text, "precisely in order to present it [...] to ensure the text's presence in the world." If poems are the text, then the paratexts are the entire apparatus—print and otherwise—that places the text in the world to be encountered by a reader, and the small press has always found interesting ways for readers to encounter texts.

The title of this book should not be misconstrued as a suggestion that the works discussed here are minor. For me, footnotes are often where the most exciting parts of texts reside. They are home to details, digressions, and contexts. They can be where things are a bit looser and more personal, and maybe a bit more fun at times. To refer to small press publications—and by extension publishers, and designers, and bookmakers—as footnotes is to embrace the excitement and freedom of the humble footnote, that which can be passed over if one isn't paying attention, but which can enrich a reading experience when used thoughtfully by writers and publishers and when considered carefully by readers.

Finally, this book—like all bibliographic labour to some degree—furnished the welcome opportunity to embrace a slower form of thinking. Some of these essays, the shortest even, took years to write. I left academia after finishing my doctorate—outside its bounds, and free from the timelines and pressures of conferences and journal publication, the work proceeded at its own pace as much as daily life allowed. I feel my thinking benefited from these conditions, even as there were days I wished I could have spent uninterrupted and unaccounted for hours looking closely at books. At this pace, I tried to pair bibliography with close reading, print history, and book design analysis of under-appreciated and under-acknowledged cultural workers—poets, publishers, artists, designers—in the service of filling in a few more pages of the records of this country's small press history.

Ottawa / you know nothing / of poems: Robert Rosewarne, Fran Jones, and the Small Press in 1960s Ottawa

> "Ottawa,
> you know nothing
> of poems
> & you are poems."
>
> — William Hawkins, *Ottawa Poems* (1966)

In 1957, Earle Birney published the article "Poets and Painters: Rivals or Partners" in *Canadian Art*, where he called for the "voluntary, even spontaneous working-together of independent artists and their poetic contemporaries." Birney decried that in North America "the two worlds have never united" and mourned that as a consequence Canada had not yet produced "the highest type of illustrated book [...] the joint work of author and artist who are contemporaries, working as in equal collaboration, inspired by similar feeling, approaching the same subject matter from opposite directions." Birney's call, while passionate, did not tell the whole story. Michele Rackham has convincingly argued against Birney's central thesis by identifying the myriad connections between poets and painters during Canada's modernist years:

> Earle Birney's accusation that the two worlds of painting and poetry "have never united" in North America is particularly perplexing, coming (as it did) at the height of the fifties [...] a decade during which Canadian Anglophone poets consistently invoked painting and the visual arts in their poetry and a revival of the "ancient and honorable union between the two arts within the covers of the same book" that Birney had called for was well under way with the small press movement.

Indeed, Rackham, surveying the works of, among others, Emily Carr, Dorothy Livesay, P.K. Page, and Betty Sutherland, argues that the "period of 1930–1960 [...] marks a period of unique collaborative and discursive activity between poets and visual artists in Canada." Here I take my cue from Rackham to examine the work of a small group of poets and artists working closely with one another in Ottawa in the early 1960s who jointly produced precisely what Birney desired—"unity of figure and design and colour and word which can turn a book into a higher entity."

In relation to Canada's 1960s small press ferment, Ottawa was a marginal hub, still, a nascent community did emerge. Although it did not prove to be as sustainable as similar scenes in Toronto, Vancouver, and Montreal, significant efforts were made by poets and artists living in Ottawa to create new conditions within which to produce and distribute explicitly collaborative work. Among the poets were William Hawkins (1940–2016), Roy MacSkimming (1944–), and Harry Howith (1934–2014). In 1963, Hawkins and MacSkimming travelled by car to Vancouver to attend the now-legendary University of British Columbia (UBC) Summer

Poetry Seminar featuring Allen Ginsberg, Robert Creeley, Robert Duncan, Charles Olson, Denise Levertov and Margaret Avison, before returning to Ottawa and promptly self-publishing a shared first collection of poetry, *Shoot Low Sheriff, They're Riding Shetland Ponies!*[3] MacSkimming would later publish a number of books, including *The Perilous Trade: Book Publishing in Canada 1946–2006* (2007), and among many other important accomplishments in Canadian publishing, was one of the founders of New Press in 1969. Howith, whose *Total War* (1967) was the final title published by Contact Press, self-published his collection *Burglar Tools* under the name Bytown Books in 1963.[4] Hawkins co-edited a little magazine, *Something Else*, which released a single issue, also in 1963.[5] Perhaps most significant for literary history—and the primary focus of this essay—are the contributions of painters and print-makers Robert Victor Rosewarne (1925–1974) and Fran Jones (1916–2002) as artists, publishers, and designers of literary works. The two ran the Blue

3 An additional component of this community regrettably beyond the scope of this essay is the role of Shirley Leishman Books, founded and operated by Bill Roberts in the late 1950s. The store stocked and promoted small-press poetry, including *Shoot Low!*, and was credited within the pages of Hawkins' later book, *Hawkins* (1965), as distributor.

4 Nicky Drumbolis, in *Zomboidgibber*, notes that *Burglar Tools* had been "conditionally accepted by the Contact Press but [was] published privately in protest to compromise." Bytown Books was announced in *Canadian Author and Bookman* 38.4 (Summer 1963): "'I suppose we're something like a co-operative,' says editor Harry Howith. 'For the time being, at least, we expect to ask most authors to contribute something towards production costs. If the book sells well enough, this will be refunded. If it keeps right on selling, we'll pay royalties. But we will not publish anything unless we believe in it.'" Bytown Books announced a second book, *That Monocycle, The Moon* by Seymour Mayne, in an issue of Louis Dudek's *Delta* in 1963 that contained Mayne's poem "Impression," but it was never published.

5 Hawkins edited the magazine with Denis Faulkner. Harry Howith and F.A. Harvey are listed as "Associates" on the masthead and Rosewarne is responsible for "Design." The magazine also earned a mention in the same issue of *Canadian Author and Bookman* as Bytown Books (Summer 1963): "As yet far from luxurious in presentation, but also commendable in content, is SOMETHING ELSE, a spirited newcomer to the periodical scene. [...] Like many another magazine in Canada, it appears to be functioning not according to the laws of economics, but on faith, hope, and precious little charity." In an email, Hawkins recalled that *Something Else* was discontinued because it was "probably too much work."

R Hand Press and Nil Press, published a series of broadside poster poems, and designed and printed books by Alden Nowlan and Al Purdy for Jay Macpherson's Emblem Books. This publishing activity was only sustained in short bursts, but it does identify the presence of a group of poets and artists looking for ways to work together in a city that generally lacked infrastructure and precedent for small press activities.[6] Furthermore, the group produced an impressively designed body of literary work, finding suitable forms for the open field, free verse poetics rising to prominence during the decade. Indeed, Nicky Drumbolis, in one of his classic small press publications, *Zomboidgibber / First Fair Letters of a User* (1991), describes Rosewarne as "an unsung genius of graphic & typographic design."

Working from Ottawa, these artists, writers, and collaborators were operating firmly on the margins of Canada's literary fields. The condition of being writers and artists—and of *making books*—from Ottawa informed the content, material production, and modes of distribution of the works, as well as their critical reception since. The works themselves were confined to a few years of intense activity (1960–63, primarily) that largely preceded the activity that has come to define formal and informal memory of the Canadian small press. The poet most closely associated with the works—Hawkins—withdrew from publishing in the 1970s, precipitating a critical silence on the literary side that in hindsight echoes the end of both Nil Press and the Blue R Hand press in the mid-1960s, when the Washington press upon which both projects relied was destroyed. These contributions to Canadian small press history have, as a result, not

6 The most nationally visible poet in Ottawa in these years was Carleton University professor George Johnston, although Johnston was publishing with Oxford University Press and thus falls outside of the small press focus of my discussion here. I do, however, possess a copy of Johnston's 1959 collection *The Cruising Auk* inscribed to Rosewarne and Jones, recording at the very least some interaction between them.

only been marginalized, but so too has Ottawa's mid-twentieth century contributions to the same.

THE BLUE R HAND PRESS

Born in Ottawa, Robert Victor Rosewarne worked as a heraldic artist at the Department of National Defense where he designed coats-of-arms, badges, and dress accoutrements. He was a founding member of the Heraldry Society and art director of the 1967 Canadian Armed Forces Tattoo.[7] Rosewarne designed sets for local theatre, was involved in puppeteer productions in Ottawa in the mid-1950s, and was an expert in the history of Canadian glass.[8] Fran Jones was born in Smiths Falls, Ontario. She worked for the federal public service in the art section of the Department of Public Printing as well as for the Queen's Printer. She graduated from the Ontario College of Art in Toronto in 1939, where she studied with Franklin Carmichael of the Group of Seven, worked at the National Film Board, exhibited in the Biennial of Prints at the Museum of Modern Art in Tokyo and Osaka, Japan, and saw her work exhibited and collected across Canada and internationally. The two were married in October 1959.

Although the works from both the Blue R Hand Press and Nil Press are primarily ascribed to Rosewarne, we know that literary history and other types of documentation often elide the contributions of women who were active participants, collaborators, and

---

7 According to W.Q. Ketchum in the *Ottawa Journal*, Rosewarne "made a notable contribution to the Tattoo presented at the Seattle World's Fair in 1967. The set he designed was 240 feet long and four storeys high. He also did the costumes, props and script diagrams."

8 One of the odder spaces on my bookshelves holds a set of six issues of *The Bottle Trail* once owned by Rosewarne. The journal was published by May Jones from New Mexico and was dedicated to the history of glass and glass collectors. Rosewarne was also "one of the first glass researchers to attempt identification of Canadian glass containers using mould numbers" according to George Miller and Elizabeth Jorgensen. Rosewarne published an article, "Canadian Base Numbers," in 1971 in the journal *Glasfax* describing his pioneering approach.

contributors. Jones' name is not cited directly in the works discussed in this essay, but in the rare instances of either press being acknowledged in print, Jones speaks on behalf of herself and Rosewarne. The two were high enough in profile to warrant regular media attention in the Ottawa press, and interviews with each undertaken during their periods of greatest activity in the small press world make it clear that they worked together. An article by Shirley Gillespie, following their wedding in October 1959, noted that the two shared a studio, and Rosewarne in 1965 noted that the two "pooled [their] studios" when speaking with W. Q. Ketchum.[9] In an article by Alex Carter published several months after Rosewarne's death, Jones describes their mutual processes of learning: "He taught me how to use the Washington press and I taught him to use colour in his work as a printmaker." My efforts in this essay are also partly to rectify the relative absence of Jones from the bibliographic notes I wrote for *The Collected Poems of William Hawkins* (2015), a project in which I did not give enough credit to Jones, owing both to the available source material that failed to acknowledge Jones sufficiently and to my own failure to recognize the familiar pattern. Jones was clearly a vital participant in the activity of both presses and I have endeavoured to locate, document, and acknowledge her contributions here.

Looking for what Melissa Dalgleish has called "a way to support the work of Canadian poetry by creating new outlets for its publication and promotion," poet Jay Macpherson started a small chapbook press named Emblem Books in 1954. Emblem ran until 1962, producing eight books in total. The published authors included—in order of appearance—Macpherson, Dorothy Livesay, Daryl Hine, Violet Anderson, Heather Spears, Dorothy Roberts, Alden Nowlan and Al Purdy. While Macpherson used local Toronto printers for the majority of the series, the books

9 The studio, initially set up by Rosewarne in 1957, was located at 317 Queen Street in downtown Ottawa on the "third floor of an old business property," and was also shared with other Ottawa artists, including Andries Hamann, according to Charles North.

by Nowlan and Purdy—*Wind in a Rocky Country* (1960) and *The Blur in Between* (1962)[10] respectively—were designed and printed by the Blue R Hand Press. Dalgleish, Canada's foremost contemporary Macpherson scholar, relays that Macpherson, "through her circle of acquaintances in Ottawa," met Rosewarne, "an extraordinarily talented printmaker" who was looking to "attempt fine literary printing." Macpherson had already accepted the Nowlan and Purdy collections for publication and turned them over to Rosewarne, who "designed colour graphics for both volumes and printed 300 copies of each." Dalgleish concludes that the two are "extraordinarily beautiful books and a far cry from the first [books] in the Emblem Books series in their design and quality."

10 In my copy of *The Blur in Between*, the publication year has been corrected in pencil from 1962 to 1963. I do not know who made this annotation, or whether it is correct.

There are few print references to the Blue R Hand. In William Toye's 1983 edition of *The Oxford Companion to Canadian Literature,* Rosewarne is mentioned in the entry on Emblem Books, but with no direct reference to the press: "Macpherson made contact in 1960 with Robert Rosewarne of Ottawa, who owned a manual letterpress [...]. A brief collaboration resulted in Emblem's two most attractive titles, each containing colour graphics by Rosewarne." The press is named directly in *Reader, Lover of Books, Lover of Heaven* (1978)—"a catalogue based on an exhibition of the book arts in Ontario compiled by David B. Kotin with a checklist of Ontario private presses by Marilyn Reuter"—and *Fine Printing: The Private Press in Canada* (1995)—a catalogue related to a traveling exhibition organized by the Canadian Bookbinders and Book Artists Guild and the Friends of the Thomas Fisher Rare Book Library. Jones, quoted directly in *Reader, Love of Books, Lover of Heaven,* provides some of the history of the Blue R Hand:

> Bob and I, both printmakers, needed a press of our own. In Westport Bob and an artist friend from the Queen Street Studios finally found the "Blue R" at the *Westport* [Ont.] *Mirror.* It was a beauty, with Greek column supports for the bed with vestiges of blue and gold paint on the name plate. It was Taylor-Washington, very similar to the one shown as William Lyon Mackenzie's in one of the Toronto Museum's publications. One of the uprights had even been smashed which unfortunately made it erratic for printing (smashed by the Family Compact and reborn as the Blue R, I fancy). Bob bought Carter's reprint of Moxon and we set to work. Jay Macpherson gave us gave us two Emblem Books to do; Bob did the illustrations for both books.

The two titles produced for Emblem Books represent the primary output of the press. *Reader, Lover of Books, Lover of Heaven* includes one additional reference to a Blue R Hand publication—the press contributed a broadside ("Street Encounter" by Harry Howith) to *Wrongfount 2: A Portfolio of Printed Pieces* issued by the Guild of Hand Printers in Toronto in 1963. Additionally, Nicky Drumbolis cites two broadsides produced under the name Blue R in 1962: "The old man and the mayflowers" by Al Purdy, produced as a promotional item for the forthcoming *The Blur in Between*, and a promotional poster for James Reaney's *Alphabet*.[11] More recently, the Purdy book appears in David McKnight's *Experiment: Printing the Canadian Imagination* (2018).

The work of Rosewarne and Jones on the two books should surely be counted alongside publications from Avrom Isaacs's Gallery Editions and Frank Newfeld's early design work at McClelland & Stewart as among the best and most successful pairings of poetry and image in Canadian literary publishing in these years, and certainly among the small press.[12] Each combines Rosewarne's colourful and abstracted prints with the poems of their respective authors. A 1960 article in the *Ottawa Journal*, written approximately at the time of publication of the two Emblem titles, describes Rosewarne as being heavily influenced

11 Drumbolis notes that the Purdy was published incorrectly under the name "Alan Purdy," and gives the title of the Alphabet poster as "life is BMQiBCFu / art is alphabet / life is also CNRJCD6V / but art is alphabet."

12 For Newfeld, I am thinking specifically of three of the four works produced for the Design for Poetry Series which incorporated a substantial number of Newfeld's original prints within the interior pages of the books: Ralph Gustafson's *Rivers Among Rocks* (1960), Leonard Cohen's *The Spice-Box of Earth* (1962), and Phyllis Gottlieb's *Within the Zodiac* (1964). That series has been the subject of excellent research and analysis by Randall Speller and requires no further discussion here (see Speller's "Frank Newfeld and McClelland & Stewart's Design for Poetry Series" in *The Devil's Artisan* 56 [Spring/Summer 2005]). Gallery Editions was run by Avrom Isaacs from his gallery, the Isaacs Gallery, in Toronto. The gallery hosted four of the five years of the first modern poetry reading series in Canada (Raymond Souster's Contact Poetry Readings) from 1957–1962, and Isaacs published three books during these same years, two of which paired a contemporary poet with a contemporary visual artist: *Eyes Without a Face* (1960), poems by Kenneth McRobbie with art by Graham Coughtry; *Place of Meeting* (1962), poems by Raymond Souster with art by Michael Snow; and *Sketch Book: Canadian and European Sketches* (1962), by Tony Urquhart.

by the English Vorticists and German Expressionists, influences that resonate with Rosewarne's design work in the two books. Although none of Jones' art appears in either book, her influence on Rosewarne can be traced to the vibrant use of colour for the prints. A 1974 review by Jenny Bergin of a show of Jones' makes clear her mastery of colour in printmaking, a skill she taught to Rosewarne as noted above: "For sheer good design and technical competence, Fran Jones' colour prints [...] must be hard to beat. With flowing, rebounding rhythms and vibrating colours, she composes visual poetry [...]" and "has exploited to the full the juxtaposition of colour and shape to which her medium lends itself so well."

In Nowlan's *Wind in a Rocky Country*, each of Rosewarne's prints is done in three colours and functions as a visual extension of the poem it decorates, creating an expression of what Birney called for (that is, artists and authors to work together "in equal collaboration [...] approaching the same subject matter from opposite directions").[13] Take, for example, Nowlan's brief poem "Summer,"

13 My copy of the Nowlan book found its way to my shelves via Hawkins and the Macpherson family. After Jay Macpherson died in March 2012, Bill was contacted by her family who had found copies of the Nil Press poster poems and the two Emblem titles published by the Blue R Hand among her belongings. Macpherson's family sent all of these to Bill, and he kindly offered me the Nowlan book.

which Rosewarne pairs with an abstracted landscape, marked by the visual evidence of his linocut technique. The work has a material quality that clearly displays the cuts and energy of its creation. The reader finds solid blue invoking both the "gray Atlantic" and the "fields at dusk" of the poem. Black and disruptive marks suggest the "rockpile" and the "broken fence," and the intense red that moves across and between echoes the movement attributed to the colt who in the final line is running "in crooked circles." Another of Nowlan's poems, "At the Fair," is similarly matched to an abstracted interpretation. Nowlan's image of two people "drenched / running to the car" and "laughing crazily" sets up the final lines:

> as the empty Ferris wheel
> went around
> and around
> in the rain.

Rosewarne's companion image suggests both the ferris wheel via a maroon half-circle pattern and the onrushing darkness of the storm through gray and black shapes.

The Purdy collection, *The Blur in Between*, is an unconventional format—it is wider than it is tall (9.75" wide by 6.5" tall)—and many of the poems occupy two columns on a single page. The prints are similar in style, though generally smaller than those in the Nowlan book. They are also, I would argue, more abstract, but still evoke connections to their poems if the reader is inclined to seek them out. Take "Night Song for a Woman," which ends with the speaker declaring that he is:

> A sound out of hearing past
> Arcturus, and still moving
> Outward: if anyone were to listen
> They'd know about humans.

The poem is paired with a print made up of an abstract pattern of sparks. Blue and purple stand out from a dark background, suggesting electricity and contact, but also stars—as Purdy's reference to Arcturus, one of the largest stars in the sky, would call for. Purdy's explicit discussion of sound and Rosewarne's image also bring to mind the visual work of Bertram Brooker, specifically his 1928 painting "Sounds Assembling." Rosewarne's work is similarly synesthetic—a visual interpretation of an aural phenomenon.

bpNichol, patron saint of the Canadian small press, cited *The Blur in Between*, and in particular the poem "Towns," as a turning point in his own reading and sense of "what was possible"—"it changed how I read and what I read." In his reflection on the title, Nichol also shares his memories of the impression that the material production of the book had on him:

> One day I'm browsing thru the poetry section in Duthie's Books when I come across *The Blur in Between* by one Alfred Purdy. It is a very beautiful book to my eyes, obviously

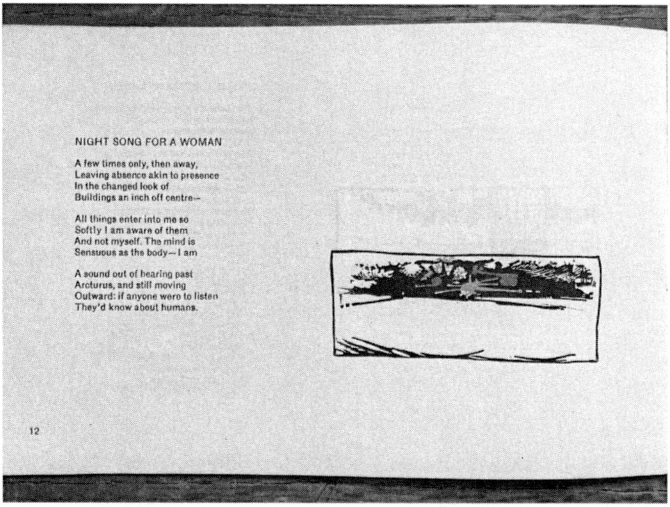

> hand set, with what look like silk-screen prints, and, when I give the pages a fast scan, the poems look good, too. It's only $1.50. This fits within my book budget, so I buy it.

I have been unable to locate any contemporary reviews of either book, but Nichol's retroactive acknowledgement of the book identifies that it at least reached the West Coast—Duthie's is in Vancouver—and that the production and price of the book were notable in the small press for their moment. Another nearly contemporary reference to the book comes from George Bowering writing about Purdy in *Canadian Literature* in 1970. Bowering cites the two Emblem Books published by the Blue R Hand as the only two titles from Emblem "spoken of much these days."

The Blur in Between is also notable for the credit it pays to Rosewarne. He is listed on the title page ("& Illustrated by R.V. ROSEWARNE")—something, I should note, that he had control over as printer of the book—and his name appears in the colophon:

> This book is published in one edition of 300 copies. It was designed by R.V. Rosewarne. The text was hand-set by Axel Harvey in 10 point Light Gothic leaded with a strip of light cardboard. The book was then hand printed on a press of the Washington variety by The Blue R Hand Press (Ottawa Canada).[14]

The colophon from *Wind in a Rocky Country* is similar—"This volume was designed and illustrated for EMBLEM BOOKS by Robert V. Rosewarne and has been hand printed in an edition of 300 copies at his R Press, Ottawa—Canada"—although the title page does not reference Rosewarne. However, despite this focus on Rosewarne, recall Jones noting that the labour of producing the books was a joint effort—"Macpherson gave *us* two Emblem Books to do" (emphasis mine).

Regrettably, as per Jones in *Reader, Lover of Books, Lover of Heaven*, "in May 1965 the studio burnt and the beautiful Blue R Press was damaged too much for our pocket book to repair." One cannot help but wonder what the press might have produced had it not been destroyed. Even the name of the press seems to have barely been settled upon before it ceased operating. In the Nowlan title, the press logo included on the colophon makes no mention of "blue" or "hand," presenting only a single letter "R" printed in blue. The Purdy book, published two years later, had a new logo clearly identifying the "Blue R Hand." It would, however, be the first and final book publication to bear the complete name.

---

14 Axel Harvey (1940–2016) was born in Montreal and studied history at Princeton. In a letter to Kenneth V. Hertz in October 1963, Rosewarne explained: "Ax the lad who was composing [...] has given up his newspaper job here and gone back to University for post-grad work." I have been unable to locate any information on Harvey beyond the above facts, which were provided by Tim Orlik.

NIL PRESS

In 1960, concurrent with the production of the two titles for Emblem Books, Rosewarne, Jones, and local artists Andries Hamann and Christopher Wells began collaborating with the young poet William Hawkins to produce a series of broadside poster poems. In emails, Wells remembers Jones and Rosewarne as the "solid, reliable adults of Ottawa's 60s art scene" and MacSkimming notes that they were "more conventional in their private lives." Conversely, poet William Hawkins was in his early twenties and little published; though he would go on to achieve some remarkable things. In addition to appearing in the seminal Raymond Souster-edited Contact Press anthology *New Wave Canada: The New Explosion in Canadian Poetry* (1966), he was published in the Oxford University Press anthology *Modern Canadian Verse* (1967) edited by A.J.M. Smith. His work appeared from Nelson Ball's Weed/Flower Press as well as in some of the most important experimental little magazines in North America, including *Alphabet, Delta, Hyphid, IS, Tish, Weed,* and *El Corno Emplumado.* He was also a creative catalyst in Ottawa's music community during the 1960s, helping to run Le Hibou, an internationally recognized coffee house, and forming and playing in a number of folk-rock bands, most notably The Children. Hawkins performed with Bruce Cockburn, Sandy Crawley, David Wiffen, Darius Brubeck, Neville Wells and others, and several of his songs were recorded by prominent Ottawa-area musicians. Hawkins' influence on Ottawa's artistic community was large at the time and has endured; indeed, Bruce Cockburn, among Canada's most celebrated songwriters, asserts that when "[he] started writing songs, it was to put music to Bill Hawkins' lyrics." Hawkins' songs were featured on the soundtrack to the 1968 NFB documentary *Christopher's Movie Matinee,* a film in which cameras were "put in the hands of a few young people [to make] this film about themselves and their world." He also organized and hosted poetry readings at Le Hibou by Irving Layton (whose reading became a spoken-word LP issued by Harvey Glatt's Ottawa record label, Posterity), James Reaney, and Gwendolyn MacEwen, and musical performances by Leonard Cohen, Gordon Lightfoot, and Joni Mitchell.

Hawkins' legacy in Ottawa was underscored by a series of books, records, and tributes in the twenty-first century. A book of selected poems, *Dancing Alone* (Broken Jaw Press) edited by rob mclennan, was published in 2005. This was followed by a tribute album, *Dancing Alone: Songs of Williams Hawkins* in 2008, courtesy of True North Records and the efforts of Harvey Glatt.[15] In 2012, Hawkins was inducted into the VerseOttawa Hall of Honour—the first poet to receive the honour—and in 2015 *The Collected Poems of William Hawkins* was published by Chaudiere Books, a book which I had the privilege of editing.[16]

Although Rosewarne and Jones' large Washington press was used to produce the two Emblem titles, it was perhaps most suited to the production of the poster poems. North's October 1960 profile of Rosewarne notes that he "acquired a press with a plate big enough to print a newspaper," and idly wonders about "what [Rosewarne] is planning for years to come." The press, and specifically its scale, allowed for the production of the poster poems, which were unique in Canadian literature at the time as far as I can tell. The posters were enormous and elaborate visual settings of Hawkins' early free verse poems printed on the Washington press via woodcut and linocut. At approximately two feet by three feet, the posters were sold for a nominal price ($0.25 to $1.00) as well as distributed for free, stapled to telephone

15 Glatt was a long-time supporter of Hawkins, as well as Ottawa's musical community more broadly. He established the Treble Clef record stores in 1957 and CHEZ-FM in 1977, among other accomplishments, and was an active and important concert promoter in the city.

16 *The Collected Poems* was published in May 2015, a little more than one year before Bill died in July 2016. Today he can be visited on Poet's Hill in Beechwood Cemetery, Canada's National Cemetery.

poles around Ottawa.[17] In addition to being early sites of contact between Hawkins and the artists who went on to illustrate his books, the posters point the way to the explosion of concrete and visual poetry that would occur across Canada in the late 1960s and early 1970s.[18] However, they were produced and distributed in Ottawa, and thus were largely off the radar of poets working in Toronto and elsewhere.

The posters were brash, exuberant, and occasionally obscene. Roy MacSkimming, recalls them as follows (in his introduction to *Dancing Alone*):

> They were also bold statements about taking poetry out of the libraries and lecture halls and sticking it in the public square, right in people's faces. As a measure of the distance society has travelled since then, particularly in the staid capital city, taking poetry to the people was an insolent, radical, unheard-of act.

derek beaulieu, writing about "political intervention" in Calgarian poetics in a 2008 issue of *Open Letter*, offers one point of entry to think about the complex politics of the poster poems. beaulieu describes a community of poets working in "linguistically disruptive forms" to articulate a "poetics of disgust" in the face of the conservative politics of Calgary, defined by its "oil and gas revenue and [...] right-wing politics." I do not intend to ascribe a similar disgust to the visual work of these artists or to Hawkins, but I do want to borrow beaulieu's placement of experimental

17 Rosewarne's biographical note in *The Blur in Between* refers indirectly to the poster poems, noting that "for several years he has devoted his time to the problems of hand printing and the production of street literature."

18 For example, the final two poster poems, "King Kong Goes to Rotterdam" and "A Song of Flowers" were designed by Christopher Wells, who provided the cover art for a number of Hawkins' published collections, including *Shoot Low Sheriff, They're Riding Shetland Ponies!* (1964), *The Gift of Space: Selected Poems 1960/1970* (1971), *Dancing Alone: Selected Poems* (2005) and *The Collected Poems of William Hawkins* (2015).

poetics in opposition to conservative politics. Ottawa, as the seat of Canadian democracy, was a site of increasing nationalist fervor as 1967 and the Centennial celebrations drew closer. 1960s Ottawa was not a place or time associated with experimental artistic work that intervened in daily civic life. The posters were the aggressive declaration of the presence and activity of an art community in an otherwise conservative city, offering a stark contrast to a municipality that had a delayed experience of the freedoms of the 1960s.

The professional public service lives of Jones and Rosewarne stand in stunning contrast to their recreational work making and distributing radical and experimental works of art. As Michelle Gewurtz notes in her essay, "Ottawa Under Pressure," the "federal government would provide many Ottawa artists with commercial opportunities in the design of stamps, currency, posters and other kinds of ephemera, which in turn sustained more experimental practices for the small but vibrant Ottawa arts community from the 1940s onwards." To think that a public servant, and one of Canada's few heraldic artists, was also responsible for printing and distributing a work like Hawkins' "King Kong Goes to Rotterdam" concisely articulates these two opposite impulses in Ottawa in the 1960s.[19] Roy MacSkimming, in an email, argues that one has to "see in the poster poems a manifestation of youthful creative energy and experimental artistic collaboration" and points to the studio of Rosewarne and Jones as one source of this because it offered a meeting place. He views the posters as an act of "rebelling against the civil servant bourgeoisie mindset of Ottawa."

Even the chosen name for the enterprise, "Nil Press," expresses this contrast: "Nil" would seem to withdraw from claiming importance or even space, but the posters themselves were stapled

19 Chris Wells and Andries Hamann also worked for the federal government. Roy MacSkimming, via email, recalls that Wells designed "Canadian government displays, often for conferences or trade fairs in the U.S. and beyond" and that Hamann designed "wildlife tableaus for the Canadian Museum of Nature."

to telephone poles for all to see. A February 1962 article by Carl Weiselberger in the *Ottawa Citizen* describes the environment in which the posters (and the two titles from the Blue R Hand) were produced: "There was a 'beatnik' touch about the creative clutter of the club, of books, bottles, easels, sculptures, but if 'beatnik' comes from being beaten, depressed and in despair, these artists are the opposite: they're serious, hard-working, optimistic people." The article also points, in somewhat poetic language, to their collaborative work and working conditions as offering a "blissful transfiguration of the prosaic roofs of Ottawa."

In total, six poster poems were published, all of poems by Hawkins.[20] The posters include little bibliographic information directly on them. Each has a title, Hawkins' name, and credits the artist—two to Rosewarne ("Two Short Ones" and "Postage Stamps"), two to Christopher Wells ("King Kong Goes to Rotterdam" and "A Song of Flowers"), and two to Andries Hamann ("Zaap" and "Rubber Boots: Canto 1"). They have most commonly been dated to 1962, but Christopher Wells places them between 1960 and 1962, noting that the two he designed were the final ones and were produced in 1962.[21]

Rosewarne's posters were most closely related to the two books printed by the Blue R Hand given the continuity of his visual style. However, whereas Rosewarne's small prints in the two

20 In addition to the above, issue number 6 of *Evidence* suggests that Roy MacSkimming was scheduled to be published in the "poster poem series," though it never happened. In an email, MacSkimming noted that "probably this was more a hope on my part than a commitment on someone else's, based perhaps on a vague suggestion by Bill [Hawkins] or Chris [Wells] or even possibly Bob Rosewarne."

21 Hawkins later published two additional large format broadsides. The first, "Sunrise: Villanelle," was published by Ottawa's S.A.W. Publications, publisher of Hawkins' final collection of the 1970s, *The Madman's War* (1974). The poem is dedicated to Andries Hamann, and the poster is bold and colourful; printed in pink, a photograph by Peter Lamb of a procession of elephants fills the broadside. No date is given, but it is most likely contemporary with Hawkins' book from S.A.W. in the mid-1970s. The second, "Still Life" (1980), was published by Patrick White's Anthos Publications coincident with the publication of the "Special/Double Ottawa Issue" of the magazine *Anthos*, which was dedicated to Hawkins.

books existed parallel to but separate from the poems, in the posters Hawkins' poems have been absorbed into Rosewarne's linocut shapes. Moreover, "Postage Stamps" and "Two Short Ones" identify how the posters—particularly in their scale, but also their aesthetics—were suited to Hawkins' work. Hawkins, in the early 1960s, the initial years of his writing life, was influenced by the Romantics and the Beat poets before exploring an open-field poetics derived from Charles Olson. Hawkins' work took seriously Olson's charge that the poet had to "get on with it, keep moving, keep in, speed [...] keep it moving as fast as you can." Hawkins' early poems often ranged across the page, rejecting a fixed left-margin to instead occupy as much of the page as possible.

"Postage Stamps" is indicative of how the posters as a complete set express a number of the contradictions at the heart of Hawkins' relationship to, and depictions of, Ottawa. In "Postage Stamps," the poet "[thinks] it's the end," declaring that he must "say something / or do something." He covers himself in postage stamps, runs through the city—a city marked clearly as Ottawa via references to "the Mall / and Bank Street too"—and cries "mail me! / mail me!" When the "crazy people" ask him "where?" he responds simply, "O anywhere." Something in Ottawa drives the poet to long for escape to "anywhere" else. Rosewarne's linocut, to my eyes, brings to mind the shape of a heart—not a cartoon heart, but an anatomically correct one. The poem pulses on the page with the speaker's discomfort.

These themes appear elsewhere in Hawkins' work, even within the restricted catalogue of the posters. "King Kong Goes to Rotterdam"—designed by Christopher Wells as a linocut—is the earliest appearance of King Kong as an avatar for Hawkins himself.[22] King Kong helps to identify elements of Hawkins' behaviour, and the persona that behaviour cultivated, which were at odds with middle-class, bureaucratic Ottawa. In "King Kong Goes to Rotterdam," the speaker has "endless aspirations of Holland," a country famous for its liberal attitudes to drugs and sex. The speaker has "seen the blond girls of Rotterdam" but must accept that he is "a billion miles" from them. Describing the King Kong poems at a reading in 1972, a reading which was later transcribed and published as the book *Northern Comfort*, the poet explained, "I sent King Kong all over the world because I couldn't go all over the world [...] at the time I wrote these, I was in jail." Hawkins' time "in jail" was a period spent at the Val Tetreau Correctional

22 Hawkins has written six poems using this monstrous King Kong persona: "King Kong Goes to Rotterdam" (1962), "King Kong Goes to Saudi-Arabia" (1962), "King Kong Meets Allen Ginsberg" (1963), "A Monster's Travelogue" (1964), "King Kong Goes to the Shawville Fair" (2005), and "King Kong Meets Godzilla" (2005). Hawkins was even depicted riding on King Kong's shoulders in Chris Wells' cover drawing for his 1971 selected poems, *The Gift of Space*, published in Toronto by New Press, in which Roy MacSkimming was a partner.

Institution in Quebec as a teenager, for what Roy MacSkimming describes as "some misdemeanor involving other people's cars." "King Kong" was a poetic outlet for impulses, behaviours, and longings, the expression of which Ottawa could not yet accommodate.[23] The poster extended the dissonance between King Kong and Ottawa by printing a naked man in graphic—if stylized—detail to be publicly displayed throughout the city.[24]

Wells also designed "A Song of Flowers," the only one of the posters produced via silkscreen instead of on the Washington press. Wells designed the poster and had the screen made "at the Exhibition Commission where I worked." In the poem, winter is "laying down endless quilts of quiet sadness" as the poet reflects on the death of his grandmother. The poem is among Hawkins' most tender and sincere on the page, despite the best efforts of the penultimate line ("And never ever a flower bloomed in sadness / lest of course it be a nutty and unserious flower"). Wells' design is suited to the poem, an animated line appearing as almost

---

23 The city did, however, celebrate Hawkins' accomplishments not too long after. In 1966, Hawkins was given an "Outstanding Young Man Award" by the City of Ottawa. Hawkins was one of three recipients, along with Russ Jackson, Ottawa Rough Riders' quarterback, and William Teron, a real estate executive credited with founding two of Ottawa's suburbs—Bells Corners and Kanata. Hawkins' coronation beside two more conventionally outstanding young men was a celebration of his distinguished service to the arts community. At the time, he had achieved a degree of publishing success, was becoming an important songwriter in Ottawa, and had recently represented Canada at the Commonwealth Festival in Wales. On the occasion of the award, the *Ottawa Citizen* called him "Canada's own Bob Dylan." Yet, this is the same era from which Roy MacSkimming characterizes Hawkins as follows: "[he] took drugs, drank too much, insulted important people. In fact he insulted most people, important or not, more or less on principle." Although he was claimed by the city through this award and held up as an "outstanding" young man presumably intended to inspire other young men to achieve outstanding feats, Hawkins' own life and artistic practice refused to conform to such an image.

24 Via email, Wells shared the following anecdote of the production of "King Kong Goes to Rotterdam": "I still have memories of us, Bill, Andries and my wife Peg, at our dining room table drinking beer while I frantically finished cutting King Kong on a linoleum block. Woodcuts and linoleum cuts have to be drawn and cut in reverse so that the printed image is readable—a challenge, particularly when you are half pissed."

a horizon, a skull, and a single purple flower appearing on the skull. Wells' two posters were the last of the six to be produced, and the use of silkscreen perhaps points to what may have been a new direction for the series had it continued.

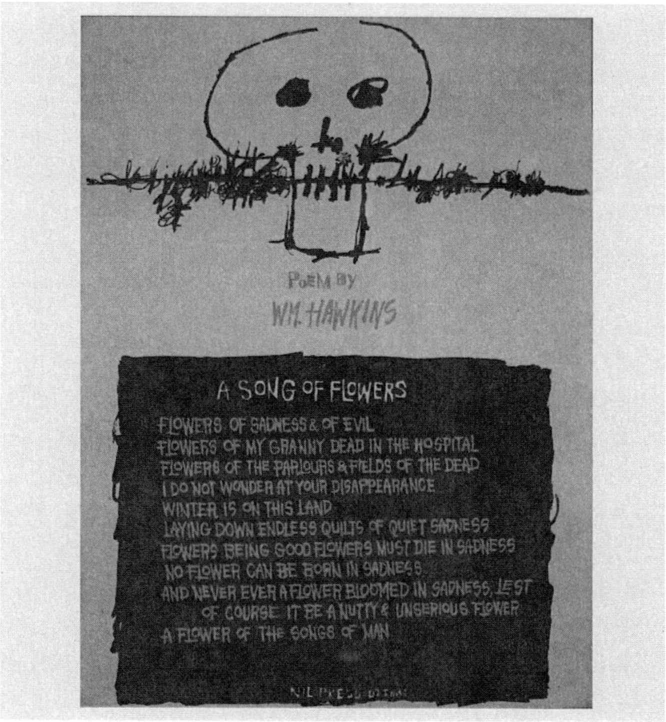

The two remaining posters—"Zaap" and "Rubber Boots: Canto 1"—were designed by Andries Hamann. "Zaap" is similar in style to Rosewarne's contributions to the series, although somewhat less lively in its linocut aesthetic. Hamann's cuts are larger—whereas Rosewarne's are fine—and the emphasis rests squarely on the poem. "Rubber Boots: Canto 1" is representational. Hamann designed a large face with an open mouth occupying the entire surface area of the poster, with the poem cut inside the open mouth. The effect is one of amplification. The poem, written in the first person, is effectively *heard* from the mouth of the figure, which is appropriate as the poem is a loud proclamation that the speaker hates "rhymes / and minor poets [...] / and mostly / lachrymose professors."

In addition to their original large format publication, the posters also made appearances in little magazines. Issue 5 (December 1962) of James Reaney's *Alphabet* included a selection of Hawkins' poems and an advertisement for the poster poems done in their characteristic style, while issue 4 (June 1962) included an effusive review of "Rubber Boots: Canto 1":

> Also a smart Interior Design grad should think of poetry wallpaper. If the rich won't buy it between covers, perhaps they'd like it on their walls. Rilke for the spare room and Ezra Pound for the counting house. Well, here's your chance! William Hawkins has come forth with a very broad, boldly and brightly designed broadsheet that would do something to any party and any room. Here is a youthful, very natural talent. With his capacity for epigram Mr. Hawkins should write a play and I hope he wallpapers a castle.

Additionally, "Postage Stamps" was reproduced in black and white in issue 18 (June 1962) of Louis Dudek's *Delta*.

Nil Press also published a small handful of additional broadsides. Nicky Drumbolis cites two other titles, each from 1962: "A strange fat little northern bird" by Milton Acorn and "the sisters" by Bill Cameron, who later became a CBC television journalist.[25]

25 After the initial publication of this essay in *DA*, Nicky kindly sent me images of these two broadsides. Each was designed by Rosewarne in a style consistent with the series as a whole and credited to Nil Press (albeit with no year of publication given on the posters directly).

Nil also published a single book, *Hawkins: Poems 1963–1965* (1966).[26] The book was designed by Rosewarne, and is well suited to Hawkins' poems. Unlike the posters which published Hawkins' open-field poetry, *Hawkins* collects narrower and tighter Creeley-esque lyric work. The book is small—4" wide and 7" tall—and, as Roy MacSkimming describes it, the poems were printed "raw in typewriter font, as if yanked straight from the manuscript." The book features a running theme along the bottom of each page of a series of colons decorating the otherwise unadorned collection. The components of the book are labelled in the running design: *half title*, *frontis*, *title*, *acknowledgements*, *contents*, and *dedication*, with the final page labeled *end*. Each verso page has "William" in the bottom right and each recto page "Hawkins" in the bottom left, so that "William Hawkins" appears at the bottom in the middle of each spread. The cover features a wraparound photograph of the poet, with Hawkins' hand holding a cigarette adorning the front cover and his face reserved for the back.

Nil Press is perhaps even less visible than the Blue R Hand Press in the written history of Canadian literature. While the Blue R Hand Press produced two books that are well-regarded and sought by collectors of the more widely-known Purdy and Nowlan, Nil Press produced only one book by a significantly less-visible poet as well as the posters which appear for sale exceedingly infrequently and are virtually unaccounted for in

26 One additional book has been attributed to Nil Press, but it was never published. In Issue 20 of *Canadian Literature*, George Bowering cites a rumour that the young poet Kenneth V. Hertz would "publish his first collection, *The Cracked Cellar*" with Nil Press. The collection was later included in George Woodcock's bibliography, *Canadian Poets 1960–1973: A Checklist*. However, Rosewarne returned the manuscript to Hertz on October 22, 1963, explaining "I am sorry but I cannot spend any more of my creative time doing other people's work [...]. All my creative time since 61 has been spent on printing others' works. I have work I have to do and so something must go and it is your book." The book was published in 1990 by Vancouver's Aleph House. A 1998 article by Robyn Sarah in the *Michigan Quarterly Review* about Hertz's health struggles noted that his "youthful poems were published for the first time" in 1990.

research collections.[27] The two original posters in my collection were found by my father at the Ottawa Antique Market in a rack of posters for sale by the daughter of a couple who were friends with Jones and Rosewarne—in other words, they were for sale well outside of the book trade. Nil does appear in Grace Tratt's *Check List of Canadian Small Presses: English Language* (1974) published by Dalhousie University as Occasional Paper 7 in their University Libraries and School of Library Service series, but even this appearance is fragmentary.[28] For each press documented, *Check List* included, where available, five pieces of information: the name of the founder(s), the date of founding, the first publication, the present or last known owners, and the present or last known mailing address. For Nil Press, the information is limited to its location—given unconvincingly as "Ottawa, Ontario (?)"—and listings for the book *Hawkins* and one of the posters, "Zaap."

The relative invisibility of the works from both presses feels indicative of Ottawa's position in the small press of the 1960s and expresses the broader marginalization faced by Ottawa's twentieth century literary and book history. Rosewarne and Jones, like Ottawa-based artists and writers before and after, paired a life of artistic production

27 All six posters are held at McMaster University in Hamilton, Ontario, while four are held at Brown University in Rhode Island and one at Carleton University in Ottawa

28 The list grew out of an earlier "major display of Canadian small press publications" hosted at Dalhousie in Spring 1971. According to series editor Norman Horrocks, research performed in order to mount the exhibition produced "a large and significant file of factual information." Tratt was Special Collections Librarian at Dalhousie at the time. Tratt completed the work that was begun by Donna Harbin Smith in 1973 and 1974 of contacting presses and collating information. At 153 pages, Tratt's *Check List* contains information on 236 small presses in varying degrees of quality and quantity. George Woodcock called it an "indispensable handbook" owing to Tratt's (and Harbin Smith's) efforts to document small presses that have been "so numerous and [...] so ephemeral" resulting in a list that, despite its gaps, was "so much more comprehensive than anything else existing." Tratt's introduction characterizes her *Check List* as "a practical working list" that "does not aim at a purist definition of small press." Rather, the scope of the *Check List* was shaped by an encompassing definition of the small press as those publishing houses which "as far as [Dalhousie] could determine, did not publish primarily for commercial purposes."

with work in the public service; their professional lives supported their artistic lives, providing a financial base from which to establish and operate their print studio. Hawkins' poetry wrestled with the limitations of being an artist in Ottawa in these years, and unfortunately, his assessment that such efforts would result in obscurity and isolation—the city, in Hawkins' book *Ottawa Poems* (1966), "extends / no hand [...] leaves me be"—proved all-too-prescient.[29] The content of Hawkins' poems, the material production and distribution of the posters, and the critical reception of the works of both presses are informed by their having been produced in Ottawa. Nonetheless, the poster poems published by Nil Press and the titles produced by the Blue R Hand Press for Jay Macpherson's Emblem Books remain today notable and successful examples of precisely what Earle Birney charged poets and painters with, namely the "joint work of author and artist who are contemporaries" to create "that unity of figure and design and colour and word."

29 Following his "retirement" in the early 1970s, Hawkins worked in relative anonymity as a cab driver until 2012, escorting the wealthy and the poor, artists and politicians, across the city, work that was equally vital but also equally underappreciated.

.edarap!: Barbara Caruso's Seripress (1972–1981) and presspresspress (1988–1998)

> "The size/shape of the page is the first decision."
> —Barbara Caruso, "Telling About Line Telling" (1973)

Barbara Caruso (1937–2009)—artist, writer, and publisher—recorded a delightful and revealing anecdote in her 1986 essay "Autobiography," describing the moment she became aware of colour. At the age of four, in the back of her family's store, she found jars of "special paints" that her sister had brought home from school to be used to make a poster: "I can still remember the flavour of curiosity that held me there. The little glass jars declared their colours. They were alive. They were beautiful." Caruso was irresistibly drawn to the "thick, rich colours" and, following her four-year-old reasoning, decided that "surely, things that looked this good must taste good." The young Caruso proceeded to taste five of the jars—the primary red, yellow, and blue, as well as white and black—and promptly fell (briefly) ill.

She would begin her life as a painter a little over a decade later at age fifteen, but this early experience seems to have left its mark on her later thinking about painting and art. In the anecdote, colour is physical. It is something to be engaged with *bodily*. Tasting the paint was an act of measuring it against her own body, against her other senses, of taking it into her body in order to understand some element of how the paint—and how the colours—existed in the world.

Caruso produced a significant body of work during her life. In addition to her primary practice as a visual artist—including but not limited to non-objective paintings exploring colour, line drawings in pencil and ink, and various engagements with letter forms—she wrote poetry and art criticism, which she published in many of the most important experimental venues in Canada, designed small press book covers for the likes of Weed/Flower Press and Coach House Press, was a collaborator with and publisher of bpNichol, and was editor and publisher of Seripress (1972–1981) and presspresspress (1988–1998). Her stated interest in the primary materials of painting—that is, paint, colour, and canvas—rather than explicit or objective representation aligned her with the exploratory nature of Canada's emerging concrete, visual, and sound poets, who were themselves interested in exploring the component parts of written language and speech. These related interests run through the range of her works but find a particularly clear expression in her work as a publisher.

In this essay, I want to bring to visibility some of Caruso's individual works of concrete poetry and situate them in relation to her other small press activities, and I also want to consider how these works and her broader work as a publisher, in their material strategies of production and distribution, are resistant to republication and remediation in print and digital forms. In particular, her considered use of the size and shape of the page, as well as her use of colour and materials, render these works difficult if not impossible to reproduce in a way that does not do fundamental damage to their original conceptions, executions, and meanings.

Caruso's first encounters with Canada's small press community came in the mid-1960s around the time of her marriage to poet, publisher, and bookseller Nelson Ball. Ball ran Weed/Flower Press from 1965 to 1974, publishing titles by bpNichol, bill bissett, David McFadden, and others. Caruso designed the majority of the book covers for Weed/Flower and contributed original artwork to collaborative publications with Ball, most notably *Points of Attention* (1971), a book that paired his characteristically minimalist poems with prints of her work. This work brought her into contact with bpNichol, who became a regular contributor to her publishing projects and a voice of support for her artistic practices.

Caruso also published a modest number of poems in the 1960s and 1970s, notable for their publication venues. She appeared in bpNichol's landmark anthology *The Cosmic Chef: An Evening of Concrete* in 1970, where one of her three contributions is the first poem in the book (or, more accurately, the box): "THE MOST DIFFICULT PART ABOUT TYPING / IS GETTING THE PAPER IN STRAIGHT."[30] This simple statement, printed at an angle to emphasize the materiality of operating a typewriter, sets the tone for the anthology. It is playful, attentive to the physical limitation of the tool she is using, and conscious of the role of the physical page in writing (and publishing) processes. Caruso also published poetry in the little magazines *Weed* and *blewointment*, and, as early as 1973, her critical writing appeared in *Open Letter*, a journal that quickly established itself as one of Canada's most significant outlets for experimental writing and writing about experimental writing.[31] Nichol solicited contributions from Caruso before editing a "Barbara Caruso" issue

30 Another of Caruso's contributions to the anthology, "earth song," is one of the only pieces to be printed in colour.

31 Caruso's first appearance in the journal was the article "Telling About Line Telling" in issue 2.5 (Summer 1973).

of the journal in 1986. The list of writers, artists, and critics who received individual issues of *Open Letter* prior to the Caruso issue is small, including Sam Perry, David Dawson, Sheila Watson, Warren Tallman, R. Murray Schafer, Louis Dudek, and Robert Kroetsch. Caruso's issue collected essays about her work, interviews, critical writings, poetry, bibliographic details, and exhibition histories. That bpNichol edited this collection is a mark of his respect for her contributions to writing and publishing in Canada and an acknowledgement of her importance to these communities.

SERIPRESS

In 1972, Caruso founded Seripress, her first publishing operation. The name emphasizes the role of her printing process and records the genesis of the project, as explained in her published journals *A Painter's Journey*: "I am thinking about printing a series of books using my silkscreen equipment. I could combine letterpress and silkscreen, like Nelson's poems and my prints, or print some of bp's concrete images. I want to call it Seripress. A silkscreen print is a serigraph; ergo, Seripress." Caruso's wealth of experience with silkscreen printing, and her particular interest in exploring colour, positioned Seripress among the Canadian small presses most capable of producing concrete and visual work. In her foreword to the Seripress fonds at McMaster University, Caruso recalls, "I was able to publish concrete or visual poetry because it was suited to the printing process, and this created opportunities to work with colour. I used colour in prints that I made to parallel some texts, and in those collaborations colour was an integral part of the visual text." The description of the Seripress collection at the University of Sheffield notes "wherever colours were used, [Caruso] mixed them herself" and quotes Caruso directly: "Silkscreen is the most direct of the print media [...] and that makes it the best medium for colour. Its directness is important to me now." For much of the work published by Seripress, Caruso filled the role of problem-solver, conceiving of ways to reproduce work that could not be as effectively printed using the dominant small-press modes of the day, such as mimeograph, linotype, or photo offset. This included her efforts to use colour as carefully and, in her own terms, as *directly* as possible.

Seripress published twenty-three titles between 1972 and 1979 before officially ceasing operations in 1981, including ten by bpNichol and three by Nelson Ball, in print runs ranging from twenty to one hundred.[32] The complete published output of Seripress resists easy categorization owing to the variety in Canadian concrete poetry in these years, and included works like the colourful experiments of bpNichol described below, minimalist work from Nelson Ball and Stephen Scobie, and other visual and concrete titles from Steve McCaffery and David Aylward. In this essay, I want to focus on the two items published by Seripress that were credited explicitly as collaborations, both between Caruso and bpNichol: *The Adventures of Milt the Morph in Colour* (1972)[33] and *H: An Excursion* (1976).[34] I focus on these collaborations for three reasons. First, they offer a contrast in scale—*Milt the Morph* used an enormous page (15" tall and 30" wide), while *H: An Excursion* was a comparably small one (6" by 6"). Second, as collaborations they allow for a consideration of how Caruso's own artistic practices interacted

32 The University of Sheffield cites twenty-one titles, while the bibliography supplied in the Barbara Caruso issue of *Open Letter* lists twenty-three "either circulated or uncirculated." The two uncirculated titles are both by bpNichol from 1971: *And Yet* and *OH*. According to the description of the Seripress collection at the University of Sheffield, "after each title was printed, the profilm stencil was dissolved from the screen, ensuring that the title could not be printed again using that original plate."

33 *The Adventures of Milt the Morph in Colour* was printed in an edition of twenty-five copies and sold for $160. Despite the higher-than-normal price for a small press title, the book sold well. On June 12, 1973, Caruso noted in her journal: "Neither bp nor I anticipated that it would sell so well. There are eight copies left now [...] with three or four sales pending [...] I have accounts receivable of almost $900."

34 *H: An Excursion* was printed in an edition of sixty copies.

with her work as a publisher. Finally, both depend explicitly on the use of colour for their meanings.

The two projects express the reciprocities between Caruso's and Nichol's practices. Caruso addresses the two titles directly in the forward to the Seripress fonds to emphasize their genesis as acts of collaboration: "In the case of the two collaborations with bpNichol, the manuscript developed through a process of exchanging ideas and was set down on paper in the form of drawings and notes that were discussed, modified, rejected or agreed upon." Indeed, the visual and literary contents of both titles explore in detail the nature of their collaborations. *The Adventures of Milt the Morph in Colour*, for example, has copious internal paratextual material. The item is a folio containing eleven leaves, consisting of a title page, a collaborative introduction, eight prints, and a colophon. The introduction contains Nichol's and Caruso's distinct voices—Nichol's presented without capital letters or conventional punctuation and Caruso's presented with both—and contextualizes the work. Nichol asserts, "what is shown is a process the coming together of two different perceptual systems at the point where they overlap where they fix around one frame of reference," while Caruso explains that the collaboration was initiated when "bp told me the shapes of the colour areas in my paintings reminded him of comic strip frames."[35]

The arrangement of the prints makes clear how the collaboration developed. The first print consists of twelve empty frames—these are Caruso's colour-shapes void of colour and/or Nichol's empty comic frames. The second print introduces Caruso's colour-shapes, the work that sparked the collaboration. In the third,

35 In Michael Ondaatje's film about bpNichol, *Sons of Captain Poetry* (1970), Nichol recalls the formative influence of comics on his own practice: "The mythology that formed part of my unconscious was comic books and comic strips [...] Comic books are the first and greatest area of borderblur." See Gil McElroy's article "Ground States: The Visual Contexts of bpNichol" for a fuller discussion of the influence of comic strips on Nichol's work.

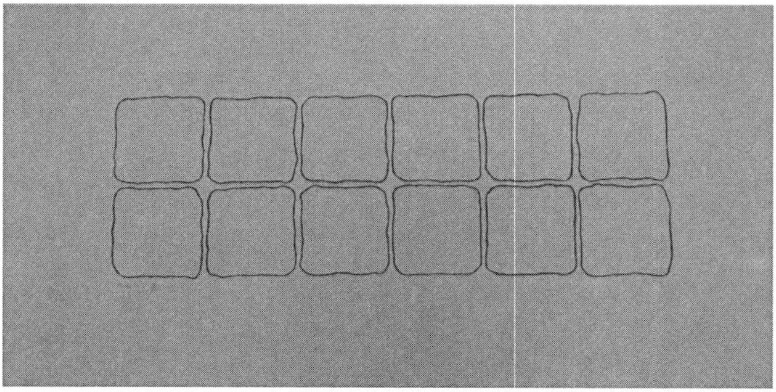

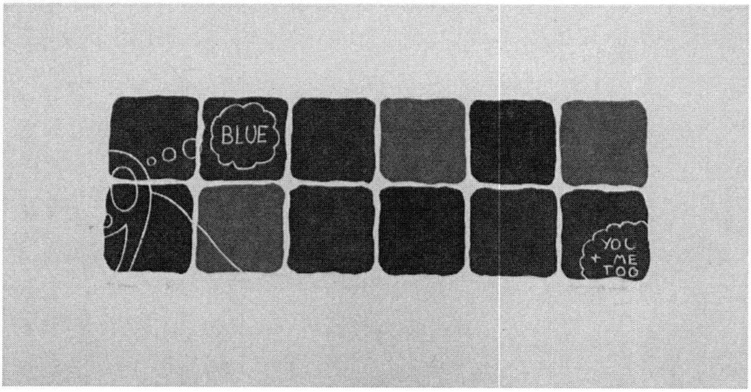

we observe the two exploring the tension between linguistic and visual representation, with the word "blue" appearing in a series of colour-shapes that are not blue. In the fourth, Nichol creates a landscape out of words ("bird," "water," "hill," "tree," and "sky" appear in the colour-shapes). Milt the Morph appears in print five with a thought bubble ("ME"). His thought, "ME," transforms into "BLUE" in print six, with an additional thought bubble in the opposite corner appearing ("YOU + ME TOO"). Finally, Milt grows out of the frames in prints seven and eight, moving further into the paper/canvas, exceeding the bounds of the print and leaving only "BLUE" and its thought bubble spread across the colour-shapes. Milt's "adventures" interact with Caruso's colours, drawing the eye to the white space (i.e., that which is *not* colour). Blue, Caruso notes in her essay "The Seripress Collaborations," was also Nichol's favourite colour: "For bp, 'blue' was a word, a sound, a name, an idea and lastly, a visual colour."

The title of the collaboration, *The Adventures of Milt the Morph in Colour*, brings Nichol and Caruso together. Milt is a recurring character in Nichol's visual work (including comics), and we know that colour was Caruso's primary concern.[36] The emphasis of the title falls on the word "in." Note in these prints that Nichol's contributions—words and drawings—are the negative space of the silkscreen print. I would also like to emphasize something that Caruso herself drew attention to in an essay about her long-running Colour Lock series of paintings: "In the Colour Lock paintings, I preserved the fact of the two-dimensional plane by leaving the canvas surface visible."[37] The Colour Lock paintings, like much of Caruso's work, insist that the viewer engage with a painting as a created object. They do not ask the viewer to lose sight of the paint or canvas in subordination to an image rendered in perfect fidelity to reality, rather they confront the viewer with their own materials—the canvas is insistently present; paint is simply paint; colour is simply colour. Milt the Morph is *in* colour; that is, he is *within* the colour, not *of* colour. Milt's presence in the work is the absence of colour and the presence of the canvas. Or in Caruso's words in "The Seripress Collaborations," "the 'white line,' being the white page, is the same as the paper margins."

The second collaboration between Nichol and Caruso, *H: An Excursion*, was published in 1976. In "The Seripress Collaborations" Caruso documents the more difficult genesis of this second collaboration.[38] The work took three years to complete as a num-

---

36 *bpNichol Comics* (2002) is a collection of comics from 1960 to 1980 that demonstrates Nichol's sustained interest in the form throughout his career, while also tracing the evolution of Milt the Morph. Editor Carl Peters argues that the earliest character in the book, Bob de Cat, "evolved into Captain Poetry—John Cannyside—St. Reat—and finally, of course, Milt the Morph."

37 The Colour Lock paintings spanned fifteen years (1969–1983) and are composed of nine related series of paintings that, as per Caruso's description in her essay about the series, "gave colour and its energy precedence over the graphic elements of the work."

38 Despite the difficulties of their collaborative relationship—and I encourage the reader to locate and read Caruso's published journals to follow in detail the evolution

ber of different ideas proved impossible, and Caruso notes that in producing *H: An Excursion*, "our different temperaments and the uneven division of labour became problematic." Although *H* foregrounds the process of collaboration in a manner similar to *Milt the Morph*, this time the collaboration followed from one of Nichol's works, not Caruso's. In her published journals, Caruso documents the moment of discovery that gave the project its final shape. Caruso wrote on January 19, 1976:

> Yesterday I went over all of the material for the collaboration with bp that I worked on last year. The overlap image that bp was enthused about is impossible. I nearly gave up; actually, I did give up. Then I found another pile of drawings that I had made in 1973 based on a planar H shape. I've never shown these to bp. Now, I see that I have taken bp's H and broken it up to develop a nine-shape Colour Lock image. Today, I have nine images, eight of which retain the H identity—only the last becomes the Colour Lock image. I like this. I'll show it to bp and see what he thinks. This may be more of a collaboration than I thought earlier, because the hand-drawn H is clearly bp's and the order of that shape invites the rest. And it invites colour. I want to print this.

Caruso did not ultimately retain all nine images in the project. *H* consists of only six prints gathered into a small folio. Nichol's contribution to the project is lesser than in *Milt*. As described above, Caruso began the work based on a drawing of the letter H

---

of these projects and of Caruso's own painting and career generally—Caruso did, on reflection, feel positively about what she learned from working closely with bp. As recorded in "The Seripress Collaborations": "I am not an easy collaborator; in fact, I am a poor one—a 'loner.' On the one hand, I am too compliant; on the other, too insistent. bp collaborated with ease and generosity. He said he liked to explore new forms of expression with others; he said that through collaborations his perception expanded. In collaboration, perceptions are shared. I learned the value of the collaborative relationship and the importance of the results from bp."

by Nichol, reproduced as the first print; the outline of the large, upper case "H" is printed in black. The second print introduces Caruso's characteristic colour to the shape. In the third print, she begins to break down the letter H into smaller colour-shapes, identifying the reciprocities between her ideas and Nichol's by reproducing his letterform using the four-sided colour-shapes she was focused on in the 1970s. The fourth print further breaks down the H and introduces more colour. The fifth print breaks the H down completely into seven colour-shapes. The final print discards the H shape and arrives at one of Caruso's Colour Lock pieces—a large square composed of nine smaller squares. Poet and critic Gil McElroy describes the initial "H" as "decaying narratively through the sequence until it becomes pure form and colour stripped of any vestigial semantic content." Moving sequentially through the prints, each image is also progressively larger by just a small amount, as though one is zooming in gradually onto the component parts of the letter. Ultimately, *H: An Excursion* is bookended by each contributor's individual work. It begins with Nichol's H and ends with Caruso's Colour Lock shapes. The rest of the material navigates the spectrum between the two; it is suspended between the poles of their individual work.

Seripress foregrounded collaboration, despite Caruso's insistence that only the two titles discussed above were collaborations. In the Nichol/Caruso collaborations, the reciprocities between Canada's emerging visual poets and Caruso's artistic practice were made explicit both in the work itself and in the paratextual apparatus that surrounds the work. Caruso notes, "it was bp who said that all Seripress books were a form of collaboration between poet and artist."[39] Conceiving of Caruso as a collaborator in all Seripress titles, as per Nichol's formulation, reveals the

39 Nichol, for example, identified another of his Seripress titles, *From My Window* (1978), as collaborative, despite Caruso not putting her own name on the title page. Nichol "made a point of saying so in print to correct the error."

essential role of the printer as a collaborator in the construction of meaning. Although Caruso initially viewed herself as simply the publisher of the works beyond the two Nichol collaborations, Nichol astutely perceived that her role was greater, and Caruso eventually acknowledged his position. The two "different perceptual systems" of the artist and poet find a common expression in these books, an expression that speaks to the particularities of Caruso's Seripress work and helps to identify the difficulties inherent in reproducing Seripress works. These collaborations show the productive potential that existed during the initial concrete ferment of these years for artists and writers to work together. Seripress was an ideal venue for these explorations, and Caruso's vital role—as designer, collaborator, publisher, and printer—has

allowed them to resist the best efforts of twenty-first-century technology to render all things immediately accessible. Following the discussion of presspresspress below, I will return to a discussion of how Caruso's work as a publisher resists such efforts.

PRESSPRESSPRESS

Caruso did not operate as a publisher again until 1988 when she launched presspresspress. She dedicated presspresspress to miniature works in miniature forms with extremely restricted distribution. Caruso published thirty-two titles through presspresspress, printed almost exclusively by rubber stamp. Unlike Seripress, presspresspress was an outlet for Caruso's own language-based work—twenty-eight of the titles from the press were by Caruso herself.[40] Although the titles span a full decade, thirty-one of thirty-two were produced between 1988 and 1990, with a single final title in 1998. Print runs ranged from ten to forty-four copies, meaning that these works were distributed in an aggressively gift-economic mode and are not widely available in research collections. Caruso did, however, keep detailed distribution notes in a handwritten notebook, where she recorded to whom copies were sent and how many were kept aside, updating the list periodically as copies were sent to new correspondents. The majority of the works were deposited in the University of Toronto Library, the National Library in Ottawa, the McMaster University Library, and the Ruth and Marvin Sackner Archive in Florida. Other copies were distributed to the likes of bookseller Nicky Drumbolis, cultural factotum jwcurry, poets and critics Douglas Barbour, Stephen Scobie, Lola Lemire Tostevin, and Paul Dutton, printer and book designer Glenn Goluska, publisher Beverly Daurio, artists Sheila Vollmer and Greg Curnoe, and Ellie Nichol, among others. Copies were also held for Caruso's own

40 A checklist of the press is provided at the end of this essay.

archive and for later distribution (derek beaulieu, for example, appears as a recipient of titles in 1999, and Nelson Ball distributed some nearly complete sets following Caruso's death).

Caruso described the initial spark for the project in a letter to jwcurry in November 1988:

> Several weeks ago I saw the exhibition of Picasso's Sketchbooks at the [Art Gallery of Ontario]. I thought it a terrific show. I began to "play" with the small sketch-cum-drawing [...] I was enjoying myself immensely, not taking myself too seriously. But, one little sketch led to another, and I began to see a kind of seriality emerge in the "play," and (you guessed it), I began to work with a passion, page after page. Then, (inherent in the word "page," notice), I turned to making little books—nothing in them, just the object. I was thrilled that I could make a little book—one staple holding so many pages, about 2" square. [...] I have begun to make little books, tiny publications under my own imprint, presspresspress.

The works of presspresspress are an engagement with the book, and specifically the *small* book, as a unit of composition. Discussing her paintings in July 1986 in the essay "Small Paintings," she wrote, "size is an element in painting. Until 1984, my paintings were large; these new works are small. In them I explore the dimensions of smallness, that particular of size, and I explore the painting as object and as surface." These words were written shortly before the printing of the first presspresspress title and indicate a developing concern with the "dimensions of smallness." The project began with Caruso's simple joy at being able to make small books, which incited her curiosity about what sorts of works they could contain, and she set about devising a new publishing project that was suited to the size and shape of the page.

Titles from the press were published in small editions with simple tools—rubber stamp and plain stickers in primary and secondary colours. The thirty-two titles include books measuring only two or three inches per side as well as a series of "broadsides" published on small sheets of paper and held in envelopes. The majority of them are near aphoristic in their brevity, many are purely visual, and some extend Caruso's interest in colour. For illustrative purposes, I am going to provide brief close readings of eight of these works. These are works that I worry about doing some damage to via this type of close reading but given the restricted availability of the texts, I will strive to describe them carefully and clearly below.

The first presspresspress title, *Study in Black and Grey* (1988), was published in an edition of ten copies. Printed via rubber stamp on translucent paper, Caruso presents the entire alphabet one letter at a time, one letter per page. The letters move around the small page, each placed in a different location, and paired with the translucent character of the paper, the letters can be read in both directions; that is, one can look forward at the letters to come, or backward at the reversed images of the previous letters. Each is printed in black but takes on different tones of grey depending on how many pages one is looking through. *Study in Black and Grey* emphasizes the sequence of the alphabet, the relation of one letter to another, and primarily focuses on the shapes of the letters, especially when looking backward through the verso page. *Study in Black and Grey* established a precedent for other presspresspress publications that would be concerned with letterforms, single words, and the implications of how they are arranged on the page/pages.

AND (1989), published in an edition of twenty-two copies, is elegant and simple. Caruso spells the title word one letter at a time on the recto pages of the book, but the work surprises the reader—as you turn the page from A to N to what you expect will be D, you instead encounter an ampersand, a stand-in symbol for the word, prior to arriving at D. In the act of spelling "and," she demonstrates the meaning of the word and performs an expansion of it. Just as the word "and" is deployed in service of the accretion and extension of meaning in language, the ampersand appears inside the word and expands it ever so slightly.

! (1989), published in an edition of nineteen copies, is the source of the odd title of this essay. The envelope presents an exclamation mark, and the cover provides half of a letter. As the reader turns the pages, the letters for "parade" march across the spread. Caruso, however, prints the letters in the order they are read, one at a time: "p" leads to "rap," which leads to "darap," and finally to the emphatic ".edarap!" One does not read *!* left to right,

but rather right to left as the pages turn and it becomes clear that the letters of "parade" are parading themselves across the page. It is a procession with the letter "r" poised in the middle as a juggler, playing with the positioning of a somewhat whimsical period that has been detached from its proper use.

A Play for Henry Moore (1989), published in an edition of nineteen copies, is perhaps the largest and most complex publication from presspresspress.[41] It is printed on a single wide sheet with five folds, creating twelve pages combined on the front and back. In *A Play*, Caruso stamps an entire upper case alphabet in a non-linear structure and decorates the letters with tiny hard-carved human figures—and a handful of dogs—exploring and climbing across the forms. I particularly like the little girl perched on top of the slanted "I," peering over the edge (perhaps looking down at the world from her own subjectivity, at all that lies beneath it). There are several dogs, as well as several additional loose periods, no longer connoting the end of something as they are required by their function as punctuation, but

41 Henry Moore was a sculptor who created abstractions of the human form.

instead free to engage more playfully with the rest of the alphabet. The "Z" comes after the final period, opening anew.

As in her painting, Caruso also explored colour deeply and thoughtfully through presspresspress. In *Citing Light: a complete work* (1990), published in an edition of thirty copies, she uses black pages to present six squares of colour in the order of a colour wheel alternating between the secondary and primary colours. The squares show the spectrum of visible light and are only activated when the book is opened and exposed to light. They are pasted onto black sheets, marked by the absence of colour and light. A related presspresspress title, *In Nature In Painting* (1988), published in an edition of fifteen copies as the second item from the press, helps to contextualize *Citing Light* as it presents a quote from Hans Hoffman that was evidently at the forefront of Caruso's thinking: "light / makes / colour / makes / light."

SKY (1990), published in an edition of sixteen copies, is one of several Caruso books dedicated to bpNichol. Again, the artist uses simple stickers, in this case seafoam or aquamarine coloured, arranged into a window shape that evokes Nichol's own *From My Window* (1978), a work published through Seripress. The window shape is created by the shape of the "sky"; it is not portrayed directly but rather is implied using the undecorated surface of the page as she so often did in her paintings. The negative space provides the frame.[42]

Perhaps the most striking of the presspresspress works is *Silence*, undated but published in 1990 and dedicated to bpNichol following his death in 1988. Wrapped in black paper with no immediately visible title—the title is in fact printed in black on the black paper—the book is printed on a semi-transparent paper that creates what Johanna Drucker calls "the doubled space of overlay." The word "hush" gives way to "shhh," which gives way to "hhhh," and finally to the capitalized letter "H." The word "silence" breaks down into a sound urging silence, followed by the lingering sound, and finally a single letter. H, famously Nichol's favourite letter, is a fitting tribute. The black wrappers take on a mournful quality as the reader is left with the silence of Nichol's loss and the lingering memory of his artistic production and influence. This book in particular does not reproduce well in photographs or in digital scans. The natural qualities of the paper, and the ability to read through the page as one turns it—both backward and forward—is key to the total meaning of the work. The words and letters linger as the "h" carries forward, just as Nichol's influence carries forward. Among the most knowledgeable readers of bpNichol and most insightful critics of Caruso, jwcurry reviewed the publication in *1cent* #271 as follows:

> this is a work of quietude so intense that it starts smoldering once it hits the cognitive level. Barbara's work rarely fails to achieve a state of total grace [...] but this one really goes beyond that. english is a pretty clunky language a lot of the time & she's managed to avoid all that, rendering the concrete liquid & the liquid vaporous.[43]

---

42 These two works also point forward to jwcurry's *MORF MY WINDOW* (2016).

43 In 2018, jwcurry reprinted *Silence* through his Room 302 Books with Nelson Ball's permission, something he had signalled interest in doing decades earlier. In *1cent* #271, published in 1991, he speculated "if [Caruso] gets enough requests, we might be able to persuade her to allow a reprint."

FORM AND REPRODUCIBILITY

Having now all too briefly examined some of Caruso's works, I want to turn to a consideration of how in Seripress and presspresspress but also in Caruso's work broadly, we encounter an artist, a set of projects, and modes of production that are resistant to reproduction. The issue is not only digital remediation but also republication in print. These works raise fundamental questions: what are the implications of republication or remediation for small works? For large works? How does scale affect reproduction? How do the original modes of production—materials, media, colour, and distribution—affect our ability to digitize or otherwise reproduce works?

Caruso's work as a painter, writer, and publisher was always exceptionally mindful about scale. The Colour Lock paintings are enormous. Seripress published works in a variety of sizes, from the uncommonly large *Milt the Morph* to small-scale broadsides, while the works from presspresspress are deliberately small in response to their rubber stamp tools and their contents. Caruso brought the same rigour to these objects that she brought to her complete artistic practice. In the article "Telling About Line Telling," she writes, "The size/shape of the page is the first decision. That activity goes on within."[44] Just as her canvas sizes were selected, the page dimensions for both presses were actively selected, and as a consequence the work is fundamentally changed via digital remediation and print republication. The collaborations with Nichol seemed to follow, at least in part, from Caruso's sense of kinship with Nichol in this understanding of size, as explained in "The Seripress Collaborations":

44 Interestingly, in the case of *H: An Excursion*, Caruso noted in "The Seripress Collaborations" that the page size was the final element to be decided but was nonetheless key to the success of the work: "I returned to the prints for the collaboration still uncomfortable about them. Something was wrong. I remember the moment when I realized what it was. On the 10" x 10" page, the excess margin was wrong. I wanted to crop each page to 6" x 6"."

> bp had a way of looking at my paintings that pleased me. At some point during conversation, he would turn to the painting on my easelboards, stand up and pace in front of it to look at it, comment, or ask a question. The fact that he stood, that he paced, measuring himself against the painting, was a physical acknowledgement of the particular of the size of the work. I believe size is an element in painting and what I saw in bp's action was a response to that.

Caruso was also resistant to allowing her paintings to be reproduced photographically for fear of the colours being changed or misrepresented, or her drawings for fear that the "dynamics of the drawings would be lost through reduction to fit the small page," as per Lola Lemire Tostevin. Her works that appear on book covers were often created specifically for book covers, for example, the cover art for Nelson Ball's 1970 Coach House title *The Pre-Linguistic Heights*, a work for which she was involved in discussions related to page size, printing, and binding, a process that allowed her to create a work suited to the book as an object and the modes of its production.[45] The original forms in which she created a work—whether a painting, drawing, or book—carry significant weight in Caruso's conception of the role of the artist and publisher. Caruso's total artistic practice shows exacting concern for the medium through which she worked and the resulting experience of the reader and/or viewer. In his 2018 reprint of *Silence*, jwcurry offered one viable option to adequately reproduce such works—he printed the work in its original dimensions and even reproduced the effect of printing in black ink on black paper. In this, however, he benefited from it being a work that did not incorporate colour. One could not successfully reproduce the colours that Caruso mixed herself for Seripress titles.

---

45 The genesis of the production of *The Pre-Linguistic Heights* is documented in the first volume of Caruso's published journals, *A Painter's Journey: 1966–1973* (2005). It was a frustrating experience, and she concludes ultimately that the "book is a disappointment."

It's important to note that the works from both presses were not mechanically reproduced. For Seripress, Caruso used the labour-intensive mode of screen printing. In her journals, she details the painstaking processes of problem-solving involved in many of these productions, including material concerns such as the mixing of colours and working with different papers, as well as aesthetic concerns related to design. For presspresspress, Caruso printed the majority of titles by rubber stamp, one impression and one copy at a time. This mode of publication is closer to handwriting a document ten or twenty or forty-four times than running a page through a mechanical printer; each page was hand cut, and each line or letter was stamped on the page individually, over and over and over. These works were demanding to produce and eschewed the emergence of more efficient tools in the 1970s and 1980s. For Seripress, Caruso made productive use of skills she developed as an artist, which were directly suited to the works of visual and concrete poetry she was publishing. For presspresspress, she selected accessible tools that allowed the playfulness of the works to be extended by the playful materials of production.

Borrowing again from Johanna Drucker, I wonder if it might be productive to think of presspresspress titles—and perhaps even Seripress titles—as closer to artists' books, wherein the book object is the primary work instead of a reproduction of a primary work. Lori Emerson distinguishes between reading interfaces that "[attempt] to erase every trace of [their] own functioning" and reading interfaces that actively rely on and engage the traces and material particularities of their functioning.[46] No title from either Seripress or presspresspress attempts to obscure its own interface. If these are reproductions, each copy is also in

46 Reading interfaces are defined by Emerson as technologies that mediate "between reader and the surface-level, human-authored writing." A printed book is a reading interface, as is a smart phone.

some fundamental way an original work done by Caruso's hand. They are also works that insist the reader see the page and recognize its contributions to the meanings of the works. Moreover, the manners of their initial productions raise still further questions, such as what variations might exist between copies? To use Walter Benjamin's language from "The Work of Art in the Age of Mechanical Reproduction," does each copy of a ten-copy edition have a unique "aura"?

Jamie Hilder notes that for concrete poetry, the "poetic form is inextricable from its distributive form," and I feel it is important to dwell on the difficulties inherent in trying to extricate poetic forms from the distributive forms of these works specifically, but also of other works of concrete poetry generally. In recent years, bpNichol has been subject to a copious amount of collection, reprint, and anthologization. The third decade of the twenty-first century is a moment of heightened visibility and accessibility for bpNichol's primary works (in 2015, his works were the subject of a feature-length film adaptation and interpretation—Justin Stephenson's *The Complete Works*—he is anthologized and taught, and a number of reprints from presses like Coach House, Talonbooks, and Book*hug keep his primary trade collections and a number of anthologies in print). And yet, the works discussed above from Seripress—works that rely explicitly on colour—are nowhere to be found, while other Nichol Seripress titles, such as *Alphhabet / Ilphabet* (1978), which was originally printed in black and white, are reproduced.[47]

In addition to issues of colour reproduction, there are issues of scale and orientation. In the case of *Milt the Morph*, the page is significantly wider than it is tall. Not only are the *Milt the Morph* prints large, but they also contain a substantial white border around the

47 Interestingly, "Ilphabet" from *Alphhabet / Ilphabet* was reproduced on the back cover of the Barbara Caruso issue of *Open Letter*, perhaps a nod by series editor bpNichol to Caruso's participation in the title as more than simply publisher.

prints, a white border that is as wide and tall as the colour-shapes that provide the frame for Milt. As quoted in the epigraph to this essay, the size and shape of the page were vital decisions for Caruso. In the case of *Milt the Morph*, the print demanded not only a large page but also a large border. Any effort to reproduce the print on a smaller page would necessitate discarding the border (i.e., discarding a key element of the work) or severely shrinking the work and rendering it difficult to engage with. Caruso's *AND* from presspresspress is instructive here—it was later republished in the one-word works issue of *Impulse* (1990) on a single page as a single word. This is vastly different than flipping through the book one page at a time and encountering each character individually. It is also different in scale—one large page compared to many small pages. The size of each letter, determined by the rubber stamp set used, relates to the page size. The meaning and joy of the piece is condensed on a single page in *Impulse*—the process of its creation by Caruso is obscured and the process of its discovery by the reader is compressed.

The works of jwcurry are clear antecedents for presspresspress, and his own efforts at reproduction provide insight. Caruso wrote to jwcurry on November 8, 1988, shortly after beginning presspresspress and explicitly noted his influence: "I cannot have done this without thinking of you for the process (rubber stamp), and both you & bp for the size." *Headz & Hez*, an anthology of the early years of jwcurry's CURVD H&z, published in 1985, three years prior to the first presspresspress publication, is illustrative. The anthology is a box holding some seventy individual objects. Each object has been painstakingly reprinted using the tools and materials of its original publication; items are printed on a variety of papers, including bus transfers and paper plates, using a variety of means, including rubber stamp and Gestetner. The seventy objects would have lost important components of poetic and distributive meaning if anthologized more traditionally. Jamie

Hilder, discussing the limits of anthologies, writes, "works that are composed on a typewriter lose the indentation that the letter makes on the page; poster poems lose their scale. [...] Three-dimensional works appear as a single, authoritative photograph; works in colour sometimes end up in black and white." Concrete and visual poetry can amplify the relations between literary or semiotic meanings and the meanings communicated by material forms of publication and distribution. Caruso was already acutely aware of such issues from her work as a visual artist, and these questions must be confronted when encountering Seripress or presspresspress.

An additional consequence of the irreproducibility of many of Caruso's works is that their place in the critical and historical record is at times misunderstood or misrepresented. David McKnight included two Seripress titles in his *Experiment: Printing the Canadian Imagination* (2018); however, he inaccurately describes Seripress as "a short-lived offshoot of Nelson Ball's mimeograph magazine *Hyphid* and his Weed/Flower Press" and as a "collaboration between Ball and his wife, visual artist Barbara Caruso." This description not only relegates the press to being an "offshoot" of a mimeograph magazine that ceased publishing four years before the first Seripress title (*Hyphid* ran for four issues in 1968), but the press was also emphatically Caruso's project. To refer to it as a "collaboration between Ball and his wife" and to frame it exclusively in relation to Ball's publishing work rather than to Caruso's artistic practice mistakenly places Ball at the centre of the project, marginalizing Caruso's labour and accomplishments.[48]

This debate, however, returns us to the problem of access, a problem that plagues readers and scholars of small press publications, particularly of more experimental works. I am not arguing

48 Another error in attribution for Seripress comes in *After Words: Visual and Experimental Poetry in Little Magazines and Small Press 1960–2025* (2025), by Steve Clay and M.C. Kinniburgh. When discussing *The Adventures of Milt the Morph in Colour*, they credit Nelson Ball with typesetting and printing the colophon, when in fact it was Nelson Adams.

that these works should not be digitized or shared in some other form that facilitates access for study or engagement or reading. However, any such process needs to be cognizant of the particular characteristics of a given work that resist remediation and reproduction. Due to their small runs, the works of Seripress and presspresspress are not overly accessible in research collections, let alone accessible for non-research-related reading. I have struggled with the question of whether my public discussion of these works is a violation in some form of Caruso's choice, at least in the case of presspresspress, to distribute these via a gift-economic mode.[49] However, the list of those to whom they were distributed suggests a carefully curated readership of peers of whom it would have been reasonable to expect an active and, to some degree, public engagement. The material conditions of their production and distribution were oriented to an existing, internal community, but a community of practitioners—Caruso distributed these works to writers, artists, and booksellers in the field. They were sent to the appropriate libraries and archives for safeguarding and otherwise shared within active circles of the like-minded as a contribution to an ongoing dialogue about poetics, production, and distribution.

In *Philosophy* (1990), a small broadside published by presspresspress in an edition of nineteen, Caruso first prints Socrates[50]—"The uncontemplative life is not worth living."—before printing her own statement—"The unexamined intuition is not worth talking about." This seems to be the key to much of Caruso's work, and of particular relevance in the context of this essay, to her works as a publisher. In the case of presspresspress, although one gets the sense that these small works arrived somewhat intuitively to Caruso, one never has the sense that she produced these works unthinkingly; despite the playfulness of many of the

49 Titles from Seripress were for sale via traditional mail-order distribution.

50 In the publication, the quote is mistakenly attributed to Aristotle.

publications, these are nonetheless serious works worked at seriously and presented to the world with astounding care. In the case of Seripress, Caruso took considerable time to find forms of publication appropriate for the concrete and visual works she was publishing. Consequently, the works from Seripress are unique in the concrete field of their era for their (often) large scale and high-quality production modes. In both presses, as in her painting, Caruso emphasized the materiality of visual art and demanded that her reader be aware of the material conditions of the work, of which size is a key element. With unparalleled rigour, these works examined issues of colour, scale, materials, and collaboration. Caruso's entire artistic practice invested significant effort examining its own material modes of production, and as such has left behind not only a rich body of work but also a body of work that continues to generate productive questions about scholarship, collection, reproduction, remediation, and access.

A PRESSPRESSPRESS CHECKLIST (Paris, Ontario)[51]

1988

1. Caruso, Barbara. *Study in Black and Grey*. 10 copies.
2. Hofmann, Hans. *In Nature In Painting*. 15 copies.
3. Caruso, Barbara. *Hand Name*. 14 copies.
4. Caruso, Barbara. *for G.S. by B.C.* 14 copies.

1989

5. Caruso, Barbara. *Pictures. Book 1*. 15 copies.
6. Caruso, Barbara. *Pictures. Book 2*. 15 copies.
7. Caruso, Barbara. *Pictures. Book 3*. 15 copies.
8. Caruso, Barbara. *!*. 18 copies.
9. Caruso, Barbara. *And*. 22 copies.
10. Caruso, Barbara. *A Play for Henry Moore*. 25 copies.
11. Caruso, Barbara. *The Princess and the Toad*. 20 copies.
12. Caruso, Barbara. *Numbers*. 24 copies.

1990

13. Caruso, Barbara. *Sheila*. 20 copies.
14. Caruso, Barbara. *Little Brown Book*. 10 copies.
15. Caruso, Barbara. *Silence*. 20 copies.
16. Caruso, Barbara. [red]. 34 copies.
17. Caruso, Barbara. *Dog. A Novel*. 21 copies.
18. Caruso, Barbara. *See Slide*. 22 copies.
19. Caruso, Barbara. *Citing Light: a complete work*. 30 copies.
20. Caruso, Barbara. *For Sheila. en francais*. Broadside #1. 14 copies.
21. Caruso, Barbara. *Star for emmett williams*. Broadside #2. 20 copies.
22. Ball, Nelson. *Rhyme*. Broadside #3. 34 copies.

---

51 Nelson Ball provided the presspresspress checklist presented here. No checklist of Seripress is presented as it has already been documented bibliographically in the Barbara Caruso issue of *Open Letter* (Sixth Series, No. 4 [Spring 1986]).

23. Caruso, Barbara. *Sky for bpNichol*. Broadside #4. 16 copies.
24. Ball, Nelson. *Words*. Broadside #5. 34 copies.
25. Caruso, Barbara. *Anti-Poetics. english version*. Broadside #6. 17 copies.
26. Aristotle and Barbara Caruso. *Philosophy*. Broadside #7. 19 copies.[52]
27. Ball, Nelson. *Sparrows*. 32 copies.
28. Caruso, Barbara. *Woon Moon. A masque*. 18 copies.
29. Caruso, Barbara. *Original Duplicate. A Blue Book*. 21 copies.
30. Caruso, Barbara. *Snow*. Broadside #8. 19 copies.
31. Caruso, Barbara. *See Sun See Saw*. 20 copies.

1998

32. Caruso, Barbara. *Against Closure: a drawing for bp*. 26 lettered copies and 18 numbered copies.

52 As noted above, although attributed to Aristotle, the quotation should be credited to Socrates.

Incomplete Field Notes: Eva Fritsch, Turnstone Press, and the Print Histories of Robert Kroetsch's "Seed Catalogue" and *Seed Catalogue*

> "Into the dark of January
> the seed catalogue bloomed
> a winter proposition, if
> spring should come, then,
> with illustrations:"
>
> —Robert Kroetsch, *Seed Catalogue* (1977)

> "The poem spreads and proliferates in its various guises."
>
> —Dennis Cooley, "On Robert Kroetsch and Turnstone" (2017)

Robert Kroetsch's "Seed Catalogue" is, as Aritha Van Herk notes, "one of the most-studied long poems in Canadian literature." A fixture of undergraduate Canadian Literature courses, it's the kind of poem that helps developing poets open their thinking about what a long poem can be—even today, nearly five decades after it was published—and it has been a rich site of study for scholars since it first appeared. There are copious response poems, peer-reviewed articles, and doctoral dissertations that address "Seed Catalogue" directly and indirectly.

When discussing it, however, we must distinguish between "Seed Catalogue" the poem and *Seed Catalogue* the book. Through four distinct editions of the book, the poem's republication in Kroetsch's *Field Notes: The Collected Poetry of Robert Kroetsch* (1981), the 1989 and 2000 editions of *Completed Field Notes: The Long Poems of Robert Kroetsch*, and innumerable anthology appearances—perhaps most notably in Coach House's influential *The Long Poem Anthology* (1979)—the print histories of both poem and book have become obscured.[53] Moreover, given the distinctive characteristics of the design and production of the first edition of the book, its print history is notably absent in existing scholarship. Originally published by Turnstone Press in 1977 as Number Seven in their Poetry Series One, the first edition was designed by Eva Fritsch, with screen-printed reproductions of seed catalogues beneath the text of Kroetsch's poem, emphasizing the already intertextual nature of the work. Fritsch's design underscored the complex relations of the poem to the seed catalogue as a historical document by rendering the catalogue present in the visual codes of the book. The particular successes of her design have never been reproduced, and this is to the detriment of our ability to read the poem.

Robert Bringhurst argues for the role of the book designer as "interpreter"—"[t]he printed page is a surface where things

53 The first three editions were published by Turnstone Press (Winnipeg) in 1977, 1979, and 1986 (reprinted in 1997) respectively, and the fourth was published by Red Deer Press (Calgary) in 2004 (with wood engravings by Jim Westergard).

inside the book and things outside the book intersect." This essay examines Fritsch's design against subsequent printings of both poem and book in order to explore how book design can support and extend the meaning of a text by engaging *things outside the book*. "Seed Catalogue" is a particularly productive text for such a study given what Kroetsch described in *The Long Poem Anthology* as the poem's concern with "the way we read the page and hear its implications," as well as its ubiquity in the field of Canadian literature. The poem is inescapable and yet, despite the book's generous first edition of 1,000 copies, is all too rarely encountered in its original form. Its conspicuous presence in the field renders it an ideal case study for the history of small press book design in Canada, and of the ways that institutional demand for affordable, large-scale reprints can degrade and obscure the original paratextual apparatus of a text, eroding possible meanings in the process.

In the absence of direct archival documents concerning the design and production of the first edition—for example, there is no correspondence in the Turnstone archives from Fritsch, Turnstone, or Kroetsch on these matters—I am instead going to draw on Kroetsch's own discussion of "Seed Catalogue" and of long poems in general, as well as on critical readings of the poem. I am building here on Julia Moss's consideration of the design of Kroetsch's earlier collection in her 1998 article, "The Particulars of Space: Looking at Robert Kroetsch's *The Ledger*." Moss traces the complex relationships between editions of *The Ledger*, examining typographic and layout changes that altered the symbolic contents of the book. Moss refers to the "creative complicity" of the publisher of the book, Applegarth Follies (operated by Michael Niederman and Hilary Bates), in constructing the meanings of *The Ledger*: "[The publisher's] presence is conspicuously evident throughout the text, to the extent that they have had an impact on the semantic effect of the poem." It is such complicity and semantic effect on the part of Fritsch and Turnstone that I want to trace here.

I am also building on Karis Shearer's study of *The Long Poem Anthology*, in which she argues that although the anthology claims to reproduce "the entire 'text'" of the long poems, including "Seed Catalogue," the texts are ultimately incomplete as they "are missing some of the radical elements [...] of their original production." Shearer notes that the critical response to the anthology has repeatedly neglected to reckon with the ways in which small presses produce "highly designed radical texts that combine visual images with the poems in a material object resistant to commodification." Furthermore, as Shearer notes, many small press books, including those collected in *The Long Poem Anthology*, were "produced collaboratively and/or had paratextual material that troubled the traditional notion of a single author." Taking up Shearer's charge, what radical elements surrounded the poem "Seed Catalogue" in its original production? What evidence of collaboration can be traced in the paratextual materials contained in the first edition of *Seed Catalogue*? And how did Kroetsch encourage and respond to these collaborative opportunities made possible by their small press context?

Eva Fritsch was born in Sweden in 1949, moved to Canada in 1958, and was a student of Fine Arts at the University of Manitoba from 1973 to 1976 where and when she crossed paths with Turnstone Press (founded by David Arnason, John Beaver, Dennis Cooley, Robert Enright, and Daniel Lenoski in the Montcalm pub near the University of Manitoba in 1976). Fritsch designed dozens of projects for the press between 1976 and 1981, including titles by Miriam Waddington, Douglas Barbour, and Ralph Gustafson, in addition to Kroetsch's *Seed Catalogue*. She also worked for *Contemporary Verse 2* and *Arts Manitoba* during those years and is currently a painter.

Kroetsch was a lifelong supporter of small presses, especially when it came to publishing his poetry. In *The* Crow *Journals* (1980), he recorded his excitement about the upcoming publication of *Seed Catalogue* in an entry from September 22, 1976, emphatically supporting Turnstone as publisher: "*Seed Catalogue* will become a book. Thanks to Turnstone Press and those four adventurers: Arnason, Cooley, Enright, John Beaver. They dare to be culture-makers, the givers of new form, in a city that prides itself on having grown old young." Kroetsch's faith in Turnstone was amply repaid by the eventual design and publication of the book but was not universally supported when he made the decision. As Dennis Cooley recalls in his essay "On Robert Kroetsch and Turnstone," "Kroetsch's support for small literary presses leads him to Turnstone. He asks Robert Enright and I one day (Sept 22, 1976) as we are dispersing from the student pub: might we be interested in publishing it? A senior professor in the Department of English registers his scorn. He will eat the manuscript if Turnstone publishes it." Despite such external 'scorn' and some production delays,[54] Kroetsch was ultimately happy with the book, and upon seeing the completed production was so pleased with Fritsch's design that he gave her his royalty cheque.

So what was it about Fritsch's design that Kroetsch responded to so positively? And why was the poem (and its author) so amenable to collaboration of this sort? Discussing the composition of the poem in an oft-quoted passage from *The Long Poem Anthology*, Kroetsch writes:

> The seed catalogue is a shared book in our society. We have few literary texts approaching that condition. I

54 The publication took longer than anticipated. Fritsch believes it was finally completed in fall 1977, fully one-year after Kroetsch recorded his excitement in his journal. In February 1977, he expressed frustration at how long it was taking, as quoted by Dennis Cooley in *The Home Place*: "I wish the rumour about SEED CATALOGUE would find its realization: but no, the book ain't out yet. I'm a believer in the local, and last fall I agreed to have Turnstone Press do a limited edition of the poem. Nothing has happened, but the manuscript is finished, complete. Perhaps it's waiting for spring, as a seed catalogue should."

> wanted to write a poetic equivalent of the 'speech' of a seed catalogue. The way we read the page and hear its implications. Spring. The plowing, the digging, of the garden. The mapping of the blank, cool earth. The exact placing of the explosive seed.

The seed is both potential and burden. It is the responsibility of the present to history and to the shared documents that connect the two. This concern with origins is common in Kroetsch's books. He is constantly excavating history and its source texts. He works with fragments, anecdotes, primary documents, tall tales, memories, and innumerable other forms of written and oral communication. We see this worked out in "Seed Catalogue" as the poet-speaker wrestles with how to be a poet in the prairies ("*How do you grow / a poet?*"). In the poem, Kroetsch is self-conscious about placing his writing in relation to other types of writing and storytelling, about how stories are told in different environments under different conditions. The poem's arrangement on the page reflects this. The text of the poem refuses the stability and clarity of the left margin and instead occupies different spaces depending on the type of material being presented. Direct quotes from catalogues, for example, always occupy the left margin, while the parts of the poem original to Kroetsch move across the page. It is a narrative poem with no single through line and a fragmented text built of multiple voices, including Kroetsch's original words, children's rhymes, the advertising copy from seed catalogues, and letters of attestation from satisfied customers. These multiple sources speak to the greater intertextual and lived environment of historical seed catalogues, Kroetsch's "Seed Catalogue," and *Seed Catalogue.*

Eva Fritsch's design of the first edition is sensitive and responsive to these ideas. The original wraps and dust jacket are restrained and minimalist, with only the title, Kroetsch's name,

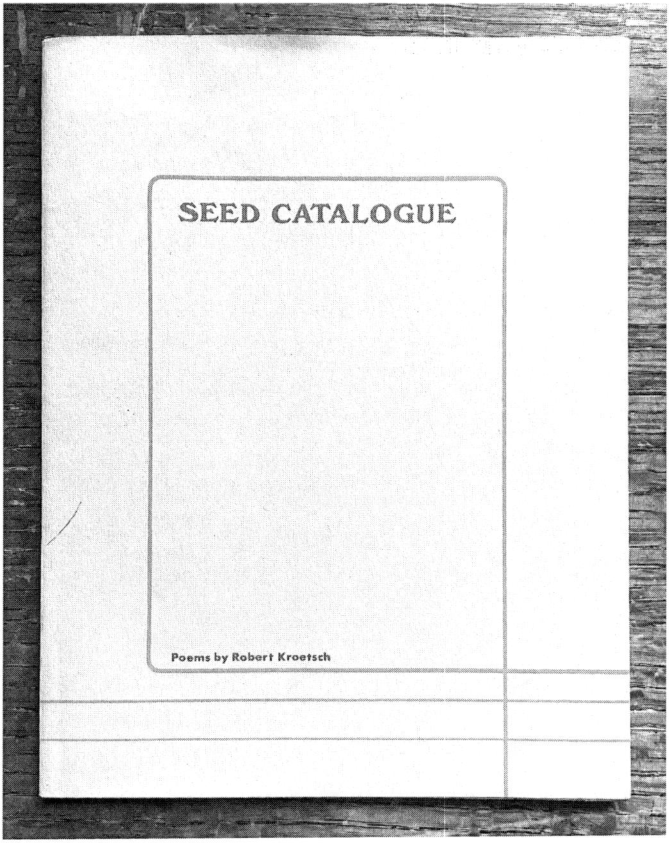

and a simple green and blue line design on a cream stock.[55] Nothing on this cover prepares the reader for what is encountered on the inside. The book designer, in Robert Bringhurst's terms, "[draws] meaning to the surface where its shape can be revealed." This is echoed in Fritsch's own description of her process in an email: "My designs all had to be in response to the poetry and after a good read of the manuscript I would come up

55 Of the original edition of 1,000 copies, 200 were hardcover and 26 of these were "lettered and signed by the author." The lettering was done by Eva Fritsch in pen and ink.

with a design [...] with Bob's manuscript I wanted to get a hold of an old seed catalogue." In the first edition, Kroetsch's poem is printed with the pages of an actual seed catalogue beneath his lines.[56]

"Seed Catalogue" was already a highly visual poem in its purely textual form, and these concerns were extended in the design of the first edition of the book. Laurie Ricou, reviewing the book in *Arts Manitoba* in 1978, describes its appearance:

> The design of the book, lovingly created by Eva Fritsch, creates another poem, or expands the possibilities of the poem. [...] The poem is printed in dark green on light, sky-blue paper. On each page, under the text of the poem, are beige silkscreens of pages from McKenzie's Seed Catalogues.

In *The Home Place*, Dennis Cooley described the catalogue images as printed "lightly in gold," not beige.[57] The ink has faded in the four decades since publication and we can now only imagine—or remember, for some—how the colours once looked. However, this loss of visual information through the gradual degradation of the printed book feels aligned philosophically with many of the concerns of the poem.

---

56 It should be noted that the screen prints are not from the original 1917 catalogue Kroetsch claims he responded to in the poem, but are nonetheless catalogues from the same company and approximately the same years—as the colophon tells us, the "screens are reproductions of pages from two McKenzie's Seeds catalogues, dated 1916 and 1922. We wish to thank Mr. William A. Moore of McKenzie Steele Briggs Seeds at Brandon for supplying them."

57 Cooley describes part of the production process: "Enright and I head over to the print shop on campus which then was publishing the Turnstone books. We look over their stock, choose a light blue paper we agree is the very thing. Eva Fritsch works on layout, carefully choosing pages from the commercial seed catalogue that resonate with the text of Kroetsch's poem, and then setting them painstakingly by hand. Why not coloured ink while were about it, when we print it? Why not? says Fritsch, and she completes the design sometime over the next several months."

Fritsch's choice to screen print seed catalogue pages beneath the poem is a visual and textual intervention in Kroetsch's work. It is comparable to some of the design work done at Coach House in the late 1960s and early 1970s, and most closely resembles Frank Davey's *Weeds* (1970) in its aesthetics.[58] *Weeds* uses a large format page—7" wide by 10.75" tall—printed in brown ink on green paper, with images of weeds printed beneath the text in green. However, in Davey's book, the intervention is purely visual. Fritsch's design for *Seed Catalogue* prints not only images from the seed catalogues, but also the advertising copy. There is more text than image in the reproductions, and this creates the possibility for Fritsch's design to intervene more aggressively in the text if the reader is interested in engaging with the design of the page.

In Fritsch's design for the first edition, the poems appear only on the recto pages while the images of the seed catalogue occupy recto and verso. The catalogue pages thus occupy more surface area of the page and more of the reader's visual field. Each part of the poem also begins on a new page—Section 2 is not placed directly under the end of Section 1, for example, but instead begins one-and-a-half pages later. This is a luxurious decision on the part of Fritsch, and a decision made exclusively for "Seed Catalogue." There are poems in addition to "Seed Catalogue" in the book, and these are printed without the images and on both recto and verso. Throughout the "Seed Catalogue" section, Fritsch also supplies page numbers only on the verso pages but supplies them on recto and verso in the other sections of the book.

In subsequent reprintings, including in editions of "Seed Catalogue" as a discrete book, the elements of the poem are compressed and constricted, making it in a more claustrophobic

58 I have heard these years at Coach House described as the "wallpaper era" as a number of books used coloured pages and images or embellishments around or under the poems, though I can find no printed source for this description. Other examples of this aesthetic on my shelves include Fred Wah's *Among* (1972), David Rosenberg's *Leavin' America* (1972), and T. Kenneth Gist's *Night* (1972).

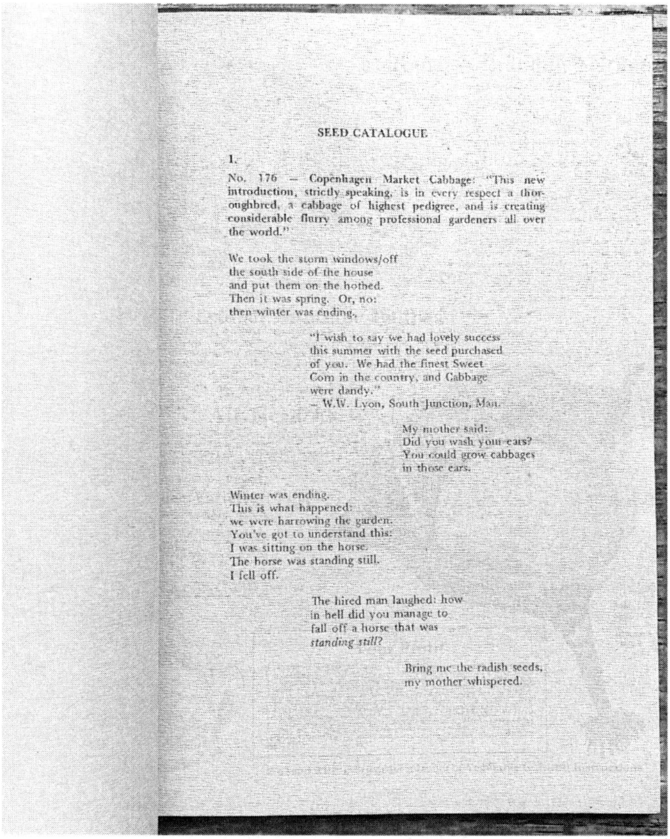

SEED CATALOGUE

1.

No. 176 – Copenhagen Market Cabbage: "This new introduction, strictly speaking, is in every respect a thoroughbred, a cabbage of highest pedigree, and is creating considerable flurry among professional gardeners all over the world."

We took the storm windows/off
the south side of the house
and put them on the hotbed.
Then it was spring. Or, no:
then winter was ending.

"I wish to say we had lovely success
this summer with the seed purchased
of you. We had the finest Sweet
Corn in the country, and Cabbage
were dandy."
– W.W. Lyon, South Junction, Man.

My mother said:
Did you wash your ears?
You could grow cabbages
in those ears.

Winter was ending.
This is what happened:
we were harrowing the garden.
You've got to understand this:
I was sitting on the horse.
The horse was standing still.
I fell off.

The hired man laughed: how
in hell did you manage to
fall off a horse that was
standing still?

Bring me the radish seeds,
my mother whispered.

work, whereas the first edition has a lovely patience in its layout and the poem itself has room to breathe. Space, the largeness of the prairies, is a focal point of "Seed Catalogue." Fred Wah, introducing the 2000 edition of *Completed Field Notes*, writes:

> ["Delphi: Commentary"] is, as are many of the poems in this book, about the imagination of place. And space. It is through poems like "Seed Catalogue," "The Sad Phoenician," "Mile Zero," and "Delphi: Commentary" that we can witness those invisible manoeuvres of our

> imagination over such large space, prairie space, sea-to-shining-sea space, frozen norths and frozen rinks, vastness. Imagine. Space with enough time to be lost.

Fritsch's design for *Seed Catalogue* embraces such conceptions of space. Her design uses a larger page than any of the later editions—the first edition is 7.5" wide by 10" tall. The 1979 second edition is smaller, measuring 6" wide by 8.5" tall, while the current in-print 1997 edition, and the one most often seen in classrooms, is smaller still, measuring 5.25" wide by 7.75" tall. The different editions of *Field Notes* run through various sizes as well—5" wide by 8.75" tall (1977), 5" wide by 8.25" tall (1989), and 6" wide by 9" tall (2000).

Section 5 of the poem—the section containing the "I don't give a damn if I do die do die do die" stanza—illustrates the effect of this choice. The section contains only 12 lines and occupies less than half of a single recto page in the first edition. Comparing the space on the page this section has, and thus the emphasis it is given in Fritsch's design, with its appearance and arrangement in later printings reveals a radically altered reading experience. In *Field Notes* (1981), Section 5 is positioned at the bottom of the recto page, towered over by the scale of the list of "absences" in Section 4. In *Completed Field Notes* (1989), it is in the middle of the verso page, wedged between the end of Section 4 and the beginning of Section 6. The effect is even more dramatic when one looks at anthologies. In *15 Canadian Poets x3* (2001), for example, the "do die do die do die" stanza is orphaned at the top of an entirely new page. The practical effect of these differences in later reprintings of the poem is an increasingly claustrophobic and rushed reading experience—in later printings, the poem fills the margins to their limits, with no space between sections.

"Seed Catalogue" exists in different contexts within its various editions in other ways too. In the first edition, "Seed Catalogue" comprises the first of three sections. It is followed by a second section of thirteen individual poems,[59] and concludes with section three, "How I Joined the Seal Herd." "How I Joined the Seal Herd" is included *Field Notes* and both editions of *Completed Field Notes*, establishing it as part of the "continuing poem," but the other thirteen poems are not collected in these later books and are actually changed in subsequent editions of *Seed Catalogue* from Turnstone. The 1979 edition makes the slight adjustment of relocating one poem within the middle section of individual poems ("Jealousy" is moved to the end of the section), and includes minor housekeeping, described by Dennis Cooley as follows: "Kroetsch writes to Marilyn Morton at Turnstone on October 30: how about cleaning up the typos in a reprint? Everyone agrees something bright and shiny is called for. On February 8 Kroetsch sends a jocular letter mocking the editors and lobbying for a sexier more sellable version. We get it out soon." The 1979 edition was redesigned without the seed catalogue reproductions, and with a new cover—the first iteration of the now-recognizable red cover with a yellow sheaf of wheat. The 1986 edition does not include "How I Joined the Seal Herd," but does include a different second section of poems under the title "Spending the Morning at the Beach."[60] This set of poems is included in the two editions of *Completed Field Notes*.[61]

The poem is obsessed with the possibilities of growth, generation, and explosion contained in the idea of the seed. As Wanda Campbell writes, "[t]he image of the seed is especially attractive to Kroetsch because of its dual potential for upward and downward movement." Campbell argues that the "energy" of the poem

59 "There is a World," "Alberta Haiku (Failed)," "Snowfall," "Getting Up to Find an Aspirin," "Conservative Streak," "Abandon Ship," "Anthem," "Historia Animalium," "Native," "Highway One," "Jealousy," "My Tree Poem," and "Identification Question."

60 "Fiji," "Brisbane," "Noosa Heads 1," "Noosa Heads 2," "Geelong," "Victoria," "Sydney," "Wellington," "New Zealand," "Rotorua," "North of Auckland," "Parry Kauri Park," and "The Hibiscus Coast."

61 The Westergard edition contains only "Seed Catalogue" and is beyond the scope of this essay. It presents new a visual reimagining and reengagement with the poem through wood engravings.

derives from the tension "between the seed full of explosive potential and the careful containment of the catalogue." These forces are present on the page in the images from the two catalogues; the language and the images that sold those possibilities are visible. The poem is also anxious about different kinds of language (think of the speaker's desire to be a "postman" delivering "real words / to real people"). The catalogue—a shared text—is a metaphor and an actual document; it holds and presents "real words" that are also acts of imagination. Semantically and visually, the catalogue presents the vocabulary of growth, survival, and nourishment that the poem dwells on and grows from. Dennis Cooley, in *The Home Place*, identifies the relationship between advertising copy, settlement, and colonization, and false promises that run through the seed catalogues and thus the poem:

> It seems right to wonder: to what extent does the embellishment [of language] derive from the propaganda that once lured settlers to the West? In it the prairies were invented as a veritable outburst of seed and blossom. The myth captivated with its promised lushness and plenitude. Superlatives and wonderfully creative language abounded.

Catalogues contributed to these processes of selling the idea of settling the West. Indeed, in a 1980 interview with Flemming Brahms, Kroetsch speculates that in "Canadian literature I'm sure you can do a thesis on the mail-order catalogue as a sub-text in terms of fantasy, of hope, of education—and depiction."

These ideas are manifest in the promises contained within the seed catalogue that are rendered visible by Fritsch's design through her use of the catalogue descriptions, the letters of attestation to the quality and success of the various seeds, and in the images of perfectly formed fruits and vegetables. In Fritsch's design, each section of the poem exists in dialogue with a carefully selected background image, creating a distinct and distinctively meaningful reading experience that can only be accessed in the first edition. In some cases, these images underscore existing and pronounced ideas from the text. In others, the images highlight Kroetsch's less overt concerns. In still others, Fritsch's choices introduce perhaps new ideas, or at least the potential for them.

Section 1, with a description of "Copenhagen Market Cabbage," is printed over top of ads for different varieties of cabbage. Prominent in the middle of the page is the claim, "All Head Early," underscoring the uncertainty between seasons and cycles of growth, decay, and regeneration that is prominent in this section of the poem: "Then it was spring. Or, no: / then winter was ending." In a poem fixated on growth and its difficulties, Fritsch's choice identifies these themes early and foreshadows the manipulation of nature and natural processes to come in the pages that follow. In some sections, Fritsch makes more literal choices that follow the text directly. For example, beneath Kroetsch's story of the speaker's father, the badger, and the potato patch in Section 2, Fritsch selects an ad for seed potatoes with an image of potatoes spilling out of a basket. Section 5 prints ads for melons beneath Kroetsch writing about melons. Section 6 prints ads for cauliflower beneath a catalogue description of cauliflower. In Section 7, Kroetsch introduces the reader to Brome Grass, his metaphor for how one grows a poet in the prairies:

> *Brome Grass (Bromus Inermis)*: "No amount of cold will kill it. It *withstands* the summer suns. Water may stand on it for several weeks without apparent injury. The roots push through the soil, throwing up new plants continually. It *starts quicker* than other grasses in the spring. *Remains green* longer in the fall. *Flourishes under absolute neglect.*"

Here, Fritsch selects an ad for "Three Great Grasses of the West," with Brome being first on the list.

Other sections of the book, however, engage with Kroetsch's text in more symbolic and expansive ways. Section 3, with a description of Hubbard Squash, is printed over different pages for Squash. Section 3 also, however, presents images of "Seed Wheat" beneath Kroetsch's descriptions of "*playing dirty*" in the granary, an image that plays on the many puns on the title throughout the poem, but more specifically on the sexual connotations of this particular section. In Section 4, Kroetsch's long catalogue of absences is printed on top of full spreads from the seed catalogue, boasting "Western Canada's Greatest Seed House," emphasizing plenty, abundance, and promise. Section 8, containing "THE LAST WILL AND TESTAMENT / OF ME, HENRY L. KROETSCH" and full catalogue spreads, reminds the reader of Kroetsch insisting that the seed catalogue is a "shared book in our society," and implies that the seed catalogue is one item that is passed between generations. The seed, from Kroetsch's poem and from the advertising copy contained in Fritsch's design, is a connection between past, present, and future, an object of commerce, of growth, of nourishment, and of textual significance.

Section 9, concerning the cousin "shot down while bombing the city that was his maternal great-grandmother's birthplace," is printed over top of ads for the chemical weapons of agriculture ("FARMOGERM," "CUTWORM KILLER") as well as ads for farm machinery that emphasize the ease of completing tasks with new, increasingly mechanized technology. This is an ironic echo of the similar application of advances in mechanization put to use during the Second World War. Section 9 in particular emphasizes the uneasy relationships within the poem between technology, growth, and destruction. The image of bundled hay in Fritsch's design evokes the shape of an exploding bomb, and can prompt consideration of Kroetsch's play on "explosion" in the book ("a bomb/exploding / in the earth / [...] It was a strange / planting.").

My discussion above has leaned more heavily on Fritsch's design than on Kroetsch's poem. I intend this as a response to the sheer volume of existing critical writing on the poem, and to attempt to establish a sense of balance between Kroetsch's poem and the particular ways it was presented by Fritsch and Turnstone Press in 1977. Kroetsch was himself thrilled with the design, and his many comments on books, bookmaking, and small presses in the 1970s demonstrate a remarkable openness to collaboration that give the reader licence to see Fritsch as a collaborator in the meaning of the poem in its first edition. In "For Play and Entrance: The Contemporary Canadian Long Poem" (1983), Kroetsch describes a "kind of madness in the recording" of Canadian long poems owing to the tension between "a) the temptation of the documentary, [and] b) the skepticism about history," noting the liberal use of "photographs, collages, analysis, protests of accuracy and source, [and] afterwords" in such books. In Kroetsch's poem, the letters of attestation and the catalogue descriptions perform this function, and in the first edition, Fritsch's design extends the textual expression of the same. Kroetsch writes that such works "[challenge] the authenticity of history by saying there can be no joined story, only abrupt guesswork, juxtaposition, flashes of insight." The interest of such poets—and Kroetsch includes himself in their number—"is in, not story, but the *act* of telling the story" and he argues that these poets produce books that "replace language with image." He declares that the poet should not be understood "as maker, but [rather as a] book-maker" and emphasizes "the book-ness of the book."

In "On Being an Alberta Writer" (1983), Kroetsch refers to the 1917 McKenzie's seed catalogue that he discovered in the Glenbow Archives in 1975 as an archaeological "deposit," and in a letter to Roy Miki explains that finding the catalogue was "like a stroke of lightning. I just knew, looking at that thing, that I had the other half of my poem. There it was, all I had to do was work it out" (quoted in Cooley, *The Home Place*). Dennis Cooley cites the two halves referred to in this quotation as *Seed Catalogue* and *The Ledger*, but I think that the terms could be more fluid than that. The catalogue itself is perhaps the 'other half' of the already-in-process poem. Regardless, Kroetsch clearly saw the two, catalogue and poem, as symbiotic. In fact, Kroetsch, in "On Being an Alberta Writer," writes that one "problem for a people who seldom see images of themselves in literature or art" is that "we fail to recognize the connection between art and life. We separate the two fatally." This fatal separation between art and life is restored to some degree in the text of the poem, but also in its design. The seed catalogue is quoted in "Seed Catalogue" textually and visually—it is insistently present.

In light of such comments, not only on the poem itself, but on the forms of Canadian long poem *books* in the 1970s, Fritsch's vital role as a collaborator in the construction of the many meanings of *Seed Catalogue* comes into focus. Julia Moss, discussing *The Ledger*, notes that Kroetsch approved of the various changes made to that poem across distinct editions: "This flexibility implies that Kroetsch allows his poem a multiplicity created by others. He resists asserting a definitive edition, even though this means a reduction of his own control over the text." Indeed, as Moss writes, "many people have laboured under the title of author," an assertion that is equally true of *Seed Catalogue*. There is further evidence of Kroetsch's openness to editorial and publishing intervention and collaboration in one of the poem's most recognizable passages:

But how –

Adam and Eve and Pinch-Me
went down to the river to swim—
Adam and Eve got drownded.

Dennis Cooley, in his retrospective narrative of the production of *Seed Catalogue*, credits David Arnason with "drownded": "Somewhere about here Arnason rereads the manuscript. The word is 'drownded,' he says. Kids say 'drownded.' 'You're right,' Kroetsch says, and changes the word on the spot." Kroetsch's approach to writing and publishing demonstrates a pattern of openness to the ideas and contributions of others and encourages a reading of the poem and book informed by its full production history.

I want to be clear that I am not suggesting that the designs of reprints and anthologies are failures on the part of editors, publishers, or designers. There are editorial, financial, and practical reasons that poems are printed in tight quarters on simple white pages. The poems are necessarily reconstituted in relation to one another in a collection like *Completed Field Notes*. *The Ledger*, for example, as outlined by Julia Moss, has its own complex print history, including a transition from a large format page to a smaller page and typographic adjustments, and yet, as Moss writes, "discourse on the interaction of text and context in *The Ledger* tends to gloss over the differences in variant editions."[62] To attempt to sustain the originality of each of these publications and produce a comprehensive volume of Kroetsch's 'continuing' works would have been impossible. However, I do want to hold up Fritsch's original design as an example of excellence in small press book design that paired text and printed book in a way that was always already nearly irreproducible. Recent reprintings from Talonbooks are instructive—Fred Wah's *Scree: The Collected Earlier Poems, 1962–1991* (2015), Daphne Marlatt's *Intertidal: The Collected Earlier Poems 1968–2008* (2017), and Phyllis Webb's *Peacock Blue: Collected Poems* (2014) take pains to reprint distinctive books as faithfully as possible given the restraints of their new material forms. In Wah and

62 The first edition is 8.25" wide by 10.25" tall, while the second edition is 6.5" wide by 7.75" tall.

Marlatt, the reader is given facsimile reproductions of coloured pages and original typesetting, while in Webb, we see an effort to reproduce significant elements of the typesetting of original publications. In the case of the Webb, I am thinking specifically of *Naked Poems*, a work with meanings that are regularly damaged in anthologies by the misrepresentation of the essential spatial and concrete elements of its composition. These efforts on the part of Talonbooks are commendable, and yet they were nonetheless constrained by the need to use a single, uniform page size.

This essay is, in part, a plea to go back as far as possible when studying small press books. The Canadian small press has a rich history of daring design work that is sometimes successful, sometimes not, but often at least tries to do something with the book that renders the reading experience distinct. Reprints, particularly once a book or poem is anthologized and absorbed into the more 'official' verse cultures of Canada, put particular material and economic pressures on a text during design and production. Clearly, it is unfeasible to reprint "Seed Catalogue" in *15 Canadian Poets x3* with the design elements of the first edition; the goal of that anthology is to be taught widely, and therefore to offer as much material as possible for as low a cost as possible. The small press, however, in a range of ways, has always resisted the imperatives of the capitalist market. What was once a small press book, or a small press poem, is something different when repackaged to serve non-small press goals.

The visual information of the first edition of *Seed Catalogue* has faded significantly in the forty years since it was published. In the two copies of the first edition I examined while writing this essay, the catalogue reproductions have faded to the point that only headings from the catalogue pages are legible. The images of seeds and their products have largely been reduced to silhouettes, and the text of the advertising copy cannot be read. The possible meanings contained in these reproductions are eroding, and many have already been lost. Moreover, one library copy I examined has been so roughly handled during its years in the stacks, and its glue has become so dried and cracked, that the pages are no longer bound and instead sit loosely between the damaged hardcover binding, held together with an elastic band. *Seed Catalogue* has become a fragile and rare edition. It could be digitized as is—and likely should be—but that would not restore the original experience of reading the first edition at the time of publication.[63] Robert Bringhurst, discussing the difficulties of photographic reproductions of books, notes that the success of such efforts is to be measured by "the degree to which they leave you uncontented with any reproduction and eager to encounter the originals instead." *Seed Catalogue* is precisely such a book, and unfortunately, the original state of its first edition is no longer intact. The poem is inescapable if one studies Canadian literature, but its print history has not been adequately recorded and the material conditions of its first edition have been lost, to the detriment of possible readings.

For the myriad academic studies of "Seed Catalogue," one rarely finds mention of Eva Fritsch's name, or discussion of the material design and production of the first edition—only Laurie Ricou's review and Dennis Cooley's writings address these issues in any depth. Scholars and readers and collectors of the small press can do more to attend to the principles that animate the material forms of such publishing work. In "Seed Catalogue" and *Seed Catalogue*, we can trace a compelling piece of Canadian small press publishing, book, and design history, but also the transition of a small press book and poem from a restricted to a general market.

63 In my experience sharing this research, the digital proved insufficient. I presented an early version of this paper during a conference ("Robert Kroetsch: Essayist, Novelist, Poet" at the University of Ottawa, April 2017). Using the projector in the room, I tried to share several images of the book, but the projected images captured none of the detail of the screen prints of the seed catalogue and so I finally opted instead to simply pass a copy of the book around the room.

In that transition, the visual signifiers of the book and poem are degraded, rendering it a different and potentially less rich poem to read. The publisher and the book designer, as mediators between reader and poem, are clearly collaborators in the production of a book's meaning. These histories need to be sought out and incorporated into more traditional textual analysis when studying the small press and small press works in Canada, and in the case of *Seed Catalogue* and other books from its era, there is an urgency to attend to these issues now as pages and ink deteriorate. There is a loss of visual context and information that, although it feels appropriate relative to the textual fragments of the poem, is nonetheless another layer, another 'archaeological deposit,' being lost. If Kroetsch's archival gesture—that is, his excavation and remediation of the seed catalogue discovered in the Glenbow archives—is significant to the poem, as existing criticism suggests, then we must acknowledge and wrestle with the archaeological gesture it was met with by Eva Fritsch and Turnstone Press during the production of the first edition of the book.

Judicious Restraint: Christine McNair and above/ground press

> "[Typography] is a craft by which the meanings of a text (or its absence of meaning) can be clarified, honoured and shared, or knowingly disguised."
>
> —Robert Bringhurst, *The Elements of Typographic Style: version 3.2* (2008)

> "Evidence is inherent in the structure of an artifact and to deny that is to slip into a kind of forgery. An erasure of what was for the sake of surface beauty."
>
> —Christine McNair, "Poetic Conservation" (2013)

In the biographical note for her second collection of poetry, the award-winning *Charm* (Book*hug, 2017), Christine McNair notes that she "lives in Ottawa, where she works as a book doctor." Book doctor is an impressive feat of understatement. Its most direct reference is to her day job—McNair is the Book Conservator at the Canadian Conservation Institute in Ottawa. Her education and training include a B.A. in English Literature with a minor in Art History from Acadia University and an M.A. in Conservation Studies from West Dean College in the United Kingdom. She completed an internship at the Centre de Conservation du Livre in France, and contracts with the London Metropolitan Archives, the Archives of Ontario, and Library and Archives Canada. Along the way she was introduced to hand-binding techniques at Gaspereau Press and the Dawson Print Shop. McNair is a poet (the author of three trade collections, as well as a handful of chapbooks, one of which was shortlisted for the bpNichol Chapbook Award), the editor of the occasional cartywheel press, owner of a private letterpress, and was the designer and co-publisher of Ottawa's (now greatly missed) trade publisher Chaudiere Books with her husband, writer rob mclennan.[64]

McNair's formal education and training are an interesting juxtaposition to mclennan's background, one of the most active writers and literary publishers in Canada for some three decades now, and likely the standalone most active on certain days. mclennan took a single post-secondary course—a poetry workshop with Mark Frutkin at the University of Ottawa in 1992–93. In the decades since, he has published innumerable books[65] and is—or has been—the editor and publisher of a dizzying numbers of

64 The final book from the press, *The Calgary Renaissance* (edited by derek beaulieu and rob mclennan) was published in 2016, and Invisible Publishing has kept the backlist available in circulation. A separate essay should be written about McNair's design work for Chaudiere. When McNair assumed her role as co-publisher in 2013, she also assumed production manager and design duties. Her design choices for the press show an admirable willingness and enthusiasm to align the form of the book object to the work. From the large scale—see Chris Turnbull's *continua*, a book measuring 9" wide by 9" tall—to the small scale—see N.W. Lea's *Understander*, a collection of poetry measuring 4.25" wide by 5" tall—her choices embrace the freedom of the small press to pursue non-standard design choices. Her work at Chaudiere has both a recognizable house style and a desire to remain adaptable to the specific needs of each project.

65 'Innumerable' is a loving exaggeration—rob is the author of several dozen trade collections of poetry, prose, and non-fiction, as well as hundreds of chapbooks.

editorial and publishing enterprises, including but not limited to *Stanzas*, *Touch the Donkey*, *ottawater*, *Peter F. Yacht Club*, Chaudiere Books, the Factory Reading Series, and above/ground press.[66]

In this essay, I am interested in exploring the ways that McNair brings her wealth of experience to bear on two anniversary publications she produced for mclennan's above/ground press. McNair's deliberate application of her book design knowledge to the history of above/ground press demonstrates an acute understanding of Jan Tschichold's injunction in "Graphic Arts and Book Design" that the job of the book designer is "to create a manner of presentation whose form neither overshadows nor patronizes the content," or, in Robert Bringhurst's formulation in the first of his "First Principles," "typography exists to honour content." Here I'll try to extend Tschichold's and Bringhurst's principles to apply more broadly. That is to say, all aspects of book design exist to honour the content of the work in question, which includes the entire book-historical content of a given project, in this case the aesthetic and print history of above/ground press as a whole.

The two objects in question were created by McNair to celebrate significant anniversaries for above/ground press—a slipcase-bound retrospective collection and bibliography of above/ground's signature poem broadsides for the 20th anniversary of the press, and an envelope-bound collection of new broadsides produced for the 25th anniversary of the press.[67] McNair's designs do not betray above/ground's firmly established house style—a cut-paste-tape-photocopy-fold-and-staple approach rooted in the early 1990s—but do accomplish an elegant engagement with that aesthetic history while reflecting the principles of typographic

66 I should note at this stage that I have benefited from the kindness and support of both McNair and mclennan over the previous decade-and-a-half in Ottawa's small press community. I have published two chapbooks with above/ground press (as well as a "poem" broadside), and a poem of mine appears in the second of the two titles discussed in this essay. Chaudiere Books also published *The Collected Poems of William Hawkins* (2015), a book I had the privilege of editing.

67 A complete list of the contents of both objects is provided at the end of this essay.

best practices. A fine press book would not have served above/ground; indeed such an approach would have been wildly out of step with the identity of the press. McNair, instead of subordinating the aesthetic history of the press to an imagined aesthetic ideal, applied her tools, skills, equipment, and knowledge to lovingly and insightfully engage with and extend the existing aesthetic project of above/ground press.

ABOVE/GROUND PRESS

Since publishing his first title under the name above/ground press—1993's *FREE VERSE ANTHOLOGY*[68]—mclennan has published more than 1,460 items through the press from a staggering cross-section of Canadian and international poets. To begin to list them would occupy more than the space available for the rest of this essay. The contributions of above/ground are significant and varied, but as these are not my focus, I will direct readers elsewhere.[69] My present interest is in the material production of chapbooks and broadsides from above/ground press.

The material aesthetic of above/ground is, like much small press publishing, a reflection of the circumstances, resources, and goals of the writer/editor. In an interview I conducted on the occasion of the 20th anniversary of the press, mclennan described his approach as follows:

68 The anthology was the first item to use the name above/ground press, but was preceded in mclennan's small press publishing history by two chapbooks of his own poetry—*LOVE & COFFEE* (1993) and *book of angels* (1993)—as well as a handful of broadsides and a brochure for a reading.

69 In 2018, when the press celebrated its 25th anniversary, mclennan published a series of essays by above/ground contributors and subscribers. I feel that these essays, more than existing interviews, reviews, or academic examinations of the press, capture the impact that the press has had during its life on writers and readers. I direct those unfamiliar with above/ground to browse the entries for a starting point to consider above/ground press: https://robmclennansindex.blogspot.com/2018/02/aboveground-press-25th-anniversary.html

> My aesthetic of the seemingly-quickly produced inexpensive photocopy and uncut pages is entirely deliberate. It initially came from my extremely low income, but also came from the idea that one didn't need to do anything expensive or complicated to get the work out. And inexpensive means I could afford to give copies away. When I think of early models of such, I am reminded of Maggie Helwig's lowlife publishing from the 1980s and early 90s. I love the rough edges of the chapbooks she used to produce. At $2 a title, I even used to purchase small handfuls (predominantly her Michael Dennis and Lynn Crosbie titles) from her at various of the Toronto Small Press Fairs to give away to friends back in Ottawa.

In the statement above, mclennan cites both an aesthetic choice—uncut pages, photocopy reproduction—and a distributive one—"inexpensive means I could afford to give copies away." To this day, mclennan lays out chapbooks with scissors and tape and uses a commercial printshop to reproduce covers and interiors. He folds and staples each item from the comfort of the home he shares with McNair, and mails out bundles of chapbooks at a rate that is frankly difficult to believe.[70]

Colin Martin, in his dissertation on Canadian chapbook presses, concisely captures the above/ground aesthetic:

> The *above/ground* press produces a very standard, ubiquitous form of chapbook. The books run from 12 pages to 32 pages (typically) in length, on regular bond paper with

70 I recall once seeing mclennan for the first time in several months, and being handed *five* subscriber envelopes containing some fifteen chapbooks. As a further illustration of mclennan's high rate of production—or perhaps my own slow rate—the earliest draft of this essay noted that the press had produced nearly 900 items whereas now the total is 1,465 as I edit the manuscript in spring 2026 (and will surely be higher by the time this book is published).

> one colour for the cover, a second for the inside flyleaf, and white printer paper for the interior, folded once to form an 8 ½ x 5 ½ page. With a single-staple saddle stitch for binding, and printed at a local commercial printer (using a laser printer or a photocopier), the above/ground chapbook is typical of low-cost, self-designed chapbooks. These are the items encountered at poetry readings and that populate book fair tables manned by young poets. The front cover often has a black-and-white image printed on it, the poems appear within various towers and cubes on the pages, and the back cover has the price and the name of the press and contact information in a format that has not changed since the 1990s.

Little has changed about mclennan's approach since he began above/ground press in 1993, whether the means or the motivation (mclennan notes, "I'd say above/ground press is unique in that I'm still utilizing the cut-and-paste method, something that I've done from the very beginnings of the press"). In an interview with Martin, mclennan even acknowledges the response he sometimes receives: "I get a lot of criticism about how my stuff looks like crap, but it's getting better and I'm actually pretty happy with how it comes out these days." It is precisely McNair's engagement with the visual codes of above/ground—codes that at times have been accused of looking "like crap"—using the depth and breadth of her formal training that I want to investigate.

Prior to participating in a panel at the International Festival of Authors (IFOA) in Toronto in 2013, McNair wrote a short article for the IFOA website that identified some of the connections between her work as a book conservator and poet. While I do not want to imply that the motivations for her design, conservation, and writing are identical, I do feel they share common philosophical grounds. As McNair writes, "My book conservation work informs my poetry writing practice in part because work with my hands balances work within my head. But there's something more direct within the book relating to how fragile and resistant the materials of the world are." She goes further and describes her book conservation in material and ethical terms, articulating her understanding of the field as "the concrete application of one's hand skills to damaged books. Or even the conscious, intelligent, judicious restraint of using one's hands." She expands on what she means by judicious restraint, noting that it can become a kind of "forgery" in book conservation to erase the physical evidence of a book or object having existed through time, what she calls an "erasure of what was for the sake of surface beauty."

Judicious restraint, a phrase borrowed for the title of this essay, is a vital principle of book design as well. Bringhurst identifies the balance that typography must strive to achieve between first drawing and second redirecting the reader's attention: "typography must often draw attention to itself before it will be read. Yet in order to be read, it must relinquish the attention it has drawn." Typography, as Bringhurst reminds us, "exists to honour content." So by looking closely at the two objects McNair produced for above/ground press, where and how can we identify McNair's expression of these balances—between fine design and the print history of above/ground, between drawing and relinquishing attention, and between applying her tools, experience, and philosophy to a press and project with a twenty-five year aesthetic and design history? In an interview conducted by derek beaulieu, mclennan states that he "had a problem with chapbooks produced in exclusive runs" to sell at higher prices, and he "found that such preciousness became self-defeating when producing a literary work that should have, first and foremost, been available to readers." And so, what does it mean to turn to techniques more commonly used for exclusive and higher-run projects to mark significant anniversaries for a press that explicitly disavows

these techniques as counter to its foundational principles? How do McNair's design choices honour and celebrate the press without disregarding the foundational principles of typography or her education and training?

THE TWENTIETH ANNIVERSARY

The first object was produced in 2013 to celebrate the 20th anniversary of above/ground press. On the colophon, it is identified as "above/ground press 20th anniversary fetish object." The fetish object is a collection of 30 of above/ground press's ubiquitous "poem" broadsides from 1999–2013, with each broadside taken from its original edition, housed in a leather and paper-bound case built by McNair.[71] It was published in an edition of 10 copies, and was available for sale at the 20th anniversary reading.[72] It is, in effect, a miniature anthology of 30 poems published by the press; however, in its construction as an object by McNair, broadsides which typically give the impression of ephemerality are more firmly fixed in time and space.

The "poem" broadsides are likely familiar to anyone who has encountered mclennan at a reading or small press book fair over the past quarter century. Each is printed on a single sheet of standard letter-sized copy paper using the full range of coloured papers available in commercial copy shops. The sheets are folded twice, as a letter would be, with the poem housed on the inside. On the outside the word "poem" appears in a design that has not changed during the life of the press, originally typed on a typewriter and then enlarged using a photocopier. It is beat-up looking, off-kilter, and fractured. The mailing address of the press appears on the other outside surface, produced in the same manner, next to the title, author, and entry number in the series. On the remaining third of the exterior surface, which is contained within the first fold, mclennan includes information on the author as well as about the press generally. As of July 2025, above/ground has produced 355 of these broadsides, representing approximately one-quarter of the total output of the press by number of titles. They are produced in large runs—typically 250-300 copies, up to 500 occasionally and 800 copies in one case—and distributed for free. They are left in public places, put on spare tables at book fairs, and handed out by mclennan and the authors. I personally use them as bookmarks within the pages of an author's books.

---

71 The collection includes a list of the broadsides, which indicates that 31 are included in the set. However, one of the planned inclusions—Max Middle's "dear jc" (#207, 2004)—was no longer available in a sufficient quantity to complete the copy edition, as explained by McNair over email.

72 The reading was held on August 23, 2013, at the Mercury Lounge in Ottawa. The readers were Marthe Reed, Gary Barwin, Marcus McCann, Wanda O'Connor and Monty Reid.

McNair's fetish object, in addition to including 30 broadsides, contains a complete bibliography of the broadside series (up to #321, July 2013), as well as a separate colophon that documents the 30 broadsides included. McNair specializes in the colophon, using the form to document her labour, to comment critically on the work in question, and to inject humour into proceedings. For the slipcase set of broadsides, her colophon is a necessary component for navigating the tension between the ephemerality of the broadsides themselves and the durability of the box within which they have been housed. She writes:

> All broadsides lightly trimmed by the butcherous bookbinder and collected into an edition of ten.[73] Each set is housed in a leather and paper slipcase. Slipcase was covered in weathered calf-skin with laid paper sides and was fancied into being by Christine McNair.

As bookbinder, McNair is "butcherous," invoking something of the violence of the enterprise. The broadsides are being removed from their natural habitat, and in the process of being contained in the slipcase, are necessarily altered. That is, they are *changed* in the process—the object is not neutral, which McNair's colophon acknowledges.

The colophon makes no direct reference to the design of the broadsides themselves, given that they were collected from their original editions and as such, did not allow McNair to perform any design—beyond the "butchery" of lightly trimming them. The bibliography and colophon, however, gesture to the full spectrum of colour that the broadsides employ. The colophon, which lists the 30 broadsides, identifies each with a bibliographic entry and a frame of the same colour as the paper used for each

73 The trimmings, if I recall correctly, were used as decoration on the book table at the 20th anniversary reading.

broadside. It is a kaleidoscopic acknowledgement of mclennan's gleeful deployment of every single colour of paper his local copy shop has on hand. The bibliography makes a similar gesture, selecting an appropriately coloured frame for each year in the series' history. Both are folded twice in the same manner as the broadsides, and presumably also trimmed by the bookbinder in order to be accommodated by the slipcase.

Despite the initial appearance of incompatibility between the slipcase and the photocopied broadsides, McNair invests her design and construction with the visual aesthetic of the original broadsides. The typewritten word "poem" and the mailing address of above/ground press appear on the paper-bound sides of the slipcase—"poem" on the front and the address on the rear. They appear precisely as they do on the broadsides, exactly as worn and damaged as they always are, and ask that the reader, who is holding a carefully constructed leather slipcase, remember that the broadsides and above/ground press are the focal point. This is where and how McNair's design and construction choices accomplish what Bringhurst calls for from the conscientious typesetter, and for my purposes, the conscientious book and book-object maker. As per Bringhurst, "the typographer's one essential task is to interpret and communicate the text. Its tone, its tempo, its logical structure, its physical size, all determine the possibilities of its typographic form." McNair had to work with not only the individual poems, but also the material manner in which these poems were published by above/ground in the past.

THE TWENTY-FIFTH ANNIVERSARY

The second object was produced in 2018 to celebrate the 25th anniversary of above/ground press. Although the second object is not explicitly identified as a fetish object, it certainly follows spiritually from the fetish nature of the first. The object is a collection of

14 broadsides, each printed on a standard-sized 8.5" by 11" sheet of coloured card stock, gathered in a standard mailing envelope. The edition size, as described in the colophon, is larger than the first fetish object: "Each broadside was produced in an edition of 150 copies. The broadsides were collected into 26 lettered sets for the authors and 114 numbered sets for general sale. The remaining 10 copies of each broadside were held for individual sale." The set includes poems by (in alphabetical order): myself, Stephanie Bolster, Stephen Brockwell, derek beaulieu, Jason Christie, Amanda Earl,

Sharon Harris, Helen Hajnoczky, Hailey Higdon, Sarah Mangold, Gil McElroy, Sandra Ridley, Chris Turnbull, and Andy Weaver.

The collection includes yet another wry and insightful colophon from McNair, playing on the tension between her formal training and the material constraints of designing an object to be produced through above/ground press:

> The broadsides were typeset in Futura and Minion by Christine McNair who takes perverse pleasure in the irritation that typeface choice may produce. There are reasons. Not the least of which is that they're hearty enough to stand up to the photocopying and she tired of weeping at disappearing serifs from prettier typefaces. She embraces the ubiquity. The two typefaces work together in a crooked way that she finds pleasing.

McNair invokes the photocopier in her explanation of design choices. The typefaces she chose had to be "hearty enough" for photocopying. If not constrained by the photocopier as the means of production, she could have chosen "prettier typefaces," but instead she embraced the constraints. Generally, Futura is used for the titles and Minion for the body of the poems, with two exceptions: my entry, "River Suite (Alexandra Bridge)," is typeset entirely in Futura, while derek beaulieu's letraset-composed visual poem is simply reproduced as it was created in an unidentified cursive typeface.

The "crooked way" the two typefaces work together invokes their disparate histories and speaks to the tension central to the fetish object. Futura is a modern, albeit older, typeface, designed by Paul Renner and released in 1927 by the Bauer Type Foundry. Bringhurst describes it as "the first and [...] best of the geometric sanserif faces" with "graceful and humane" proportions. Minion, in contrast, was designed by Robert Slimbach and issued in the late 20th century (1989) by Adobe—that is to say, for digital use. Minion is described by Bringhurst as "economical" and "fully developed," and is in fact the typeface used to set *The Elements of Typographic Style*. In the crooked meeting of the two typefaces, the reader encounters something of the history of type design, from casting in metal type to the digital revolution. Although the two faces were released only six decades apart—a small fraction of the 500-year history of moveable type—they nonetheless span an era-defining shift in the tools for both designing and setting type.

The colophon includes an image of a ship from an antique coin, depicting a type of antenna (the velata antenna) used to control ships during a storm or battle.[74] Perhaps this image spoke to McNair as a designer facing a battle between her formal training, instincts, and personal tastes, and the limitations of the photocopier as the mode of production. Indeed, the broadsides bear the mark of the photocopier, demonstrating McNair's final embrace of its conditions of production. The broadsides are slightly off balance, slanted, at times too close to the edge of the page, surely a result of images shifting slightly during reproduction. The toner—toner, not ink—has the not-quite-settled effect common to the photocopier and desktop printer that's ubiquitous in the 21st century; it is on the surface of the page, not absorbed or pressed deeply into it. I highlight these characteristics not as problems or failures of design, but rather as entirely in keeping with the material and design history of above/ground press. They even invoke mclennan's principle, quoted earlier, of prioritizing a low cost-per-unit and ease of distribution: "the idea that one didn't need to do anything expensive or complicated to get the work out [...] inexpensive means I could afford to give copies

74 I emailed McNair to ask if the image was, as I originally thought, Odysseus tied to the mast. I was thinking that Odysseus was perhaps a proxy for the designer who hears the siren call of fine press work and design but knows these practices would be wrecked on the shores of the photocopier. Alas, McNair replied that was not the intention, but I nonetheless document my initial thought here.

away." The photocopier, a machine that creates inexpensive and low-quality reproductions in large volumes, is a synecdoche for both the degradation of craft and production values in the 20th century as well as the freedoms and potential to create it holds in the right hands.

Despite her overtures to the photocopier, McNair does bring an element of handcraft to the project. As noted on the colophon, the "envelopes were individually stamped with gold foil using a Kwikprint" (specifically, "ABOVEGROUND 25" was stamped). The Kwikprint is a foil-stamping machine, first produced in 1926 coincident with the design and release of the Futura typeface. Like the photocopier, however, there is an interesting tension between the Kwikprint as an item designed to be used for business purposes and its subsequent adoption by the small press.[75] The goal of the Kwikprint was to personalize goods—leather goods originally—and it is still in production today. The tabletop model is advertised as the "perfect machine for imprinting napkins, ribbons, leather name tags, small scrapbook albums, stationary, plastic name badges, bibles, military badges and much more!" In principle, however, it clearly bears a significant resemblance to a printing press, including the requirement to handset type (albeit in brass, not lead). The machine's ability to stamp leather, to say nothing of the visual and aesthetic possibilities of simple foil stamping, perhaps rendered its adoption by printers and publishers inevitable.

Whereas in the first fetish object McNair could do no actual typesetting or design for the broadsides themselves, the second fetish object provided her with full control. Each broadside contained within the envelope is printed in black with a design that evokes elements of each poem. The designs vary from the geometric, abstract and minimal (see Hailey Higdon's

75 Toronto's late, great Ferno House (2009–2013) was known to foil-stamp their press logo on the back of chapbooks.

"The Day" or my own "River Suite [Alexandra Bridge]") to the more representative and objective (see Jason Christie's "no quarter"). The images, of course tailored to the poems, also feel in step with the overall project. There is a sustained visual motif of cross-sections and diagrams. In these images—of a thing sliced open, of the fossil record, of a schematic diagram—the reader is reminded that the object is itself a cross-section of the impressively varied bibliography of above/ground press. We are seeing an unrepresentative slice, because no slice could capture twenty-five years of activity and more than 1,000 publications. The broadsides from Helen Hajnoczky, Andy Weaver, and Sandra Ridley appear to depict fossilized remains; Amanda Earl's entry shows a diagrammatic cross-section of a human head focusing on the mouth and the machinery of speech[76]; while Gil McElroy's poem includes a diagram of Canadian storm signals from the early-twentieth century. Sharon Harris' "Grammar Queen" uses a semaphore diagram for the letter "P," a specialized and restricted mode of communication that relies on the body to communicate meaning across distance, which is appropriate to Harris' poem since it's about a body wearing letters in multiple forms. Other broadsides trade visually in the language of nature so often used to describe the gift economy in the Canadian small press, such as Stephanie Bolster's "TASHME (Sunshine Valley)" which uses an image of a root system.

There is a visual coherence to the set of broadsides, despite how they vary individually from one another. This is accomplished via the consistent use of typefaces, but also via the mode of production. The use of a photocopier with only black toner provides a clear and unified visual identity. Perhaps counter intuitively, this coherence is also supported by the use of a broad

76 Amanda Earl's broadside is also the only one with printing on both sides. The poem in question is relatively brief, but includes 35 notes that McNair chooses to present on the back of the broadside.

Sandra Ridley

Anomalocaris

I ache sometimes from loving the Burgess Shale in the Canadian Rockies, this one exceptional preservation of thousands, fossils of complicated creatures, they're unequivocal—no evidence each derived from simpler ancestors. I love those with eyes stationed above their proboscis, feelers in a drift of the sudden appearance of forms. Found diversions from the record of what we would expect to see—stones turned, faith evolving from the steam of the eucalyptus of the meeker. Out of the heat, Anomalocaris, I too love with teeth and spiked claws. We first big predators as hunting began—yes, we with armored fists—finally us—each need, credo, a long sorrow in our eyes. In fact, these lenses are crystalline. Fearless, more of us would see—yes, we as prey with soft tactics, we animals, voracious in stasis, in change, with our hallelujah eyes. Here, we do go swimming, and oh, I do love you, Anomalocaris, with your sophisticated compound eyes—what do we look for, before the word erased—fiat, genesis, Kicking Horse Pass. We look for our geological blink, for no evidence these eyes evolved at all—each of our eyes, formed abruptly, completely—and some of us with partly formed legs, and some of us with partly formed eyes, some of us with partly formed tails, free swimming, some of us with partly formed defenses, protective shells—are we fit enough to survive with hard parts for protection—I love the whole range of us, remnants, we fossils—I too love without—the last spider crab, the shrimp, the lobster, and these sea-horses alive in my chest—we horses, first of the deep Cambrian Sea, before these cliffs. Preserved and particular, abnormal, beyond taxonomy, each beside each—we in coping postures—curled in deposits. Burgess Shale, beds, burrows and track-ways—backs arched upwards, and others of us in similar catastrophes. Yes, our seafloor was quite steep before the flood of mudstone and faith buried each of our soft bodies alive.

Typeset in Minion and Futura by Christine McNair for the above/ground 25th anniversary broadside series.

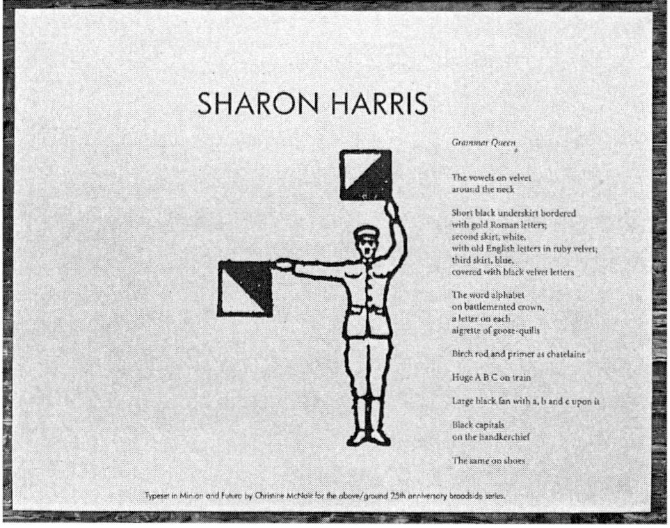

SHARON HARRIS

Grammer Queen

The vowels on velvet
around the neck

Short black underskirt bordered
with gold Roman letters;
second skirt, white,
with old English letters in ruby velvet;
third skirt, blue,
covered with black velvet letters

The word alphabet
on battlemented crown,
a letter on each
aigrette of goose-quills

Birch rod and primer as chatelaine

Huge A B C on train

Large black fan with a, b and c upon it

Black capitals
on the handkerchief

The same on shoes

Typeset in Minion and Futura by Christine McNair for the above/ground 25th anniversary broadside series.

range of available cardstock colours—there is a wide spectrum of colour (none is repeated), just as the collection contains a wide spectrum of poetics. As with the twentieth anniversary fetish object, the enthusiastic use of coloured paper is in keeping with the above/ground's house style.

There can be an element of the unforgiving and the prescriptive in statements concerning excellence in typography and design. Tschichold, for example, insisted in "Clay in a Potter's Hand" (1949) that "[g]ood taste and perfect typography are surprapersonal"; that in "a masterpiece of typography, the artist's signature has been eliminated"; and that "[g]ood typography can never be humorous. It is precisely the opposite of an adventure." Bringhurst leaves more room when he argues, half a century later, that typography must make "visual sense and historical sense" and invites readers of *The Elements of Typographic Style* to "break the rules, and break them beautifully, deliberately, and well." The rules, indeed, are not enough. When Bringhurst cites "historical sense" his intended reference is to the "history of letterforms and their usages," but I think we can learn from McNair that the broader print and aesthetic history of the subject of the book must also be accounted for, and that these histories, however anterior to the established rules for typographic excellence they may be, can justify disregarding the rules as well as potentially injecting personal and even humorous elements.

Describing her conservation work in an interview with Sandra Ridley, McNair explains that she strives to "follow the path of other pairs of hands that put particular things together and try to assess the meaning and structure inherent in the artifact. Each one contains its own node of insistent truth and persistent identity." In the same interview, she describes her private bookbinding and edition work as "separate and unique" in relation to her conservation work, but in the case of these two fetish objects, I feel there is significant overlap. The "insistent truth and persistent identity" of above/ground press infuses every element of these two objects, and in the case of the first object in particular there are elements of the archive and of conservation in the act of building a slipcase to house objects from the press' past. Regardless, although these two objects are not perfectly analogous to conservation, McNair's philosophy of "conscious, intelligent, judicious restraint" and her resistance to the "erasure of what was for the sake of surface beauty" are unquestionably present in the design and production of each.

Bringhurst writes that the typographer must "make the visible relationship between the text and other elements (photographs, captions, tables, diagrams, notes) a reflection of their real relationship." Again, Bringhurst confines his discussion to the setting of type on the page, and the other elements to which he refers are similarly confined to the page in his formulation. I feel that the clarity of his principles, however, contains breadth for my interpretation. The "other elements" are precisely the point of my discussion of McNair's specific choices in these two fetish objects. Even the term *fetish object* gestures knowingly at the contrast between the dominant above/ground visual aesthetic and the fact of the press producing such objects. above/ground is thoroughly resistant to the fetishistic—in modes of production and distribution—that characterize one corner of the small press literary field. The two objects, despite being clearly identified as standing outside of the primary body of the press's bibliography, navigate this tension masterfully, binding together the at-times disparate philosophies of mclennan and McNair. They are exceptional—that is, *exceptions* to the primary body of work of the press—but do not turn their backs on either the history of the press or its own distinctive modes of production.

CONTENTS OF THE TWO FETISH OBJECTS

above/ground 20th anniversary fetish object featuring a selection of "poem" broadsides from 1999–2013 as well as a bibliography of poem broadsides published by the press from 1995–2013[77]
(Ottawa: above/ground press, [2013])

1. Greg Evason, "just thinking again" (#95, 1999)
2. kath macLean, "madame sings orange butterflies" (#99, 1999)
3. derek beaulieu, "portrait 4" (#101, [1999])
4. rob mclennan, "stones & ice: a translation" (#116, 2000)
5. Laurie Fuhr, "It Must be the End of the World, Because..." (#121, 2000)
6. Steven Heighton, "MIXED TAPES" (#189, 2003)
7. Suzannah Showler, "springes to catch woodcocks" (#203, 2004)
8. ross priddle, "double dose" ([#204], [2004])
9. nathalie stephens, "Held (abrēgē)" (#216, [2004])
10. Peter Norman, "BOLSHEVIK TENNIS" (#218, 2004)
11. Kristina Drake, "Sex at 31" (#226, [2005])
12. Gwendolyn Guth, "The dimensions of the entreprise are such" (#232, 2005)
13. Mari-Lou Rowley, "2 CosmoSonnets" (#235, 2005)
14. Shauna McCabe, "physical geography" (#238, [2005])
15. George Bowering, "untitled" (#241, [2005])
16. Gil McElroy, "Sure Points & Lubricants" (#248, [2006])
17. Carla Milo, "Cone" (#269, [2007])
18. kevin mcpherson-eckhoff, "every six seconds..." (#273, 2008)
19. Phil Hall, "Newlove" (#274, [2008])
20. Robert Majzels, "from 85" (#275, 2008)
21. Priscila Uppal, "The Old Debate of Don Quixote vs Sancho Panza"

77 As noted, the bibliography included in the box itself indicates that Max Middle's "dear jc" (#207, 2004) is included, however it was no longer available in a sufficient quantity to complete the copy edition and so is not present in the box. As such, it is not included in the checklist here.

(#280, [2008])
22. derek beaulieu, "wild rose country" (#285, [2009])
23. Sandra Ridley, "Plunge" (#286, [2009])
24. Pearl Pirie, "Helene relates" (#287, [2009])
25. Stephanie Bolster, "NIGHT ZOO" (#289, [2009])
26. Marilyn Irwin, "This side of pyr | ryp foe dis siht" (#306, [2012])
27. Jamie Bradley, "Sex at 31" (#307, [2012])
28. Nick Ravo, "A Boab in Broome, Western Australia" (#308, [2012])
29. Natalee Caple, "Robert Kroetsch" (#311, [2012])
30. Sonnet L'Abbé, "Influence" (#316, [2013])
31. "above/ground press 'poem' broadside bibliography 1995–2013"

above/ground 25
(Ottawa: above/ground press, [2018])

1. Cameron Anstee, "River Suite (Alexandra Bridge)"
2. Stephanie Bolster, "TASHME (Sunshine Valley)"
3. Stephen Brockwell, "Above Ground"
4. derek beaulieu, [untitled]
5. Jason Christie, "no quarter"
6. Amanda Earl, "I think with my lips,"
7. Sharon Harris, "Grammar Queen"
8. Helen Hajnoczky, "pink skies #1"
9. Hailey Higdon, "The Day"
10. Sarah Mangold, "from '*Her Wilderness Will Be Her Manners*'"
11. Gil McElroy, "JD 2457299 (Blue)"
12. Sandra Ridley, "Anomalocaris"
13. Chris Turnbull, "brilliant"
14. Andy Weaver, "from Cleave"

Tactile Language: Jessica Bebenek's *k2tog*

> "We can find in the origins of the word 'text' itself some support for extending its meaning from manuscripts and print to other forms. It derives, of course, from the Latin *texere*, 'to weave,' and therefore refers, not to any specific material as such, but to its woven state, the web or texture of the materials."
>
> —D.F. McKenzie, *Bibliography and the Sociology of Texts* (1986)

> "Material form becomes meaningful form through design, that is, through considered relationships."
>
> —Anni Albers, *On Weaving* (1965)

The small press in Canada occasionally produces a book that asks its reader to dismantle it to some degree. Perhaps most infamous is bpNichol's *Cold Mountain* (1966), a chapbook that included instructions for its own literal destruction by fire.[78] *Cold Mountain* is

78 As per jwcurry, Nichol's chapbook was "an early sculptural concrete poetry

an extreme example, but it does point to a recurring small press impulse to put the book-object to work to expand the meaning of a text and to draw the reader into a more tactile reading experience.[79] Dismantling does not, however, need to take such a destructive form. Think of Steve McCaffery's *Carnival*, a work that asks to be deconstructed as a book and reconstructed as a large-scale poster in its own instructions: "In order to destroy this book please tear each page carefully along the perforation. The panel is assembled by laying out pages in a square of four." The subject of this essay—Jessica Bebenek's *k2tog* (2018)—directs this same energy towards encouraging the reader to consider handcraft, community, and a feminist and physical engagement with a body of poetry, all the while confronting the question of the integrity of the object of the book.

Jessica Bebenek is a Montreal-based artist, writer, and bookmaker. She holds a degree in English and Creative Writing from York University (Toronto) and an MA in English from Concordia University (Montreal). She writes poetry, fiction, and non-fiction and has been widely published in Canada, with a first trade collection, *No One Knows Us There*, appearing from Book*hug in 2025. She previously ran the Toronto-based small press Grow & Grow, and most germane to this essay, works at the Centre for Expanded Poetics at Concordia, an interdisciplinary research space that includes a workshop dedicated to book production (digital and analog). At the Centre, Bebenek is a Risograph printer and bookmaker.

Bebenek's experimental and feminist poetic, artistic, and publishing practices find one of their many sites of overlap in her k2tog series. To discuss k2tog is to discuss a standalone book, an

book/object" with instructions to bend the pages to form loops before dropping a lit match into the middle loop and incinerating the whole thing.

79 Another element of this impulse beyond the scope of this essay is to make objects that prod at the tendency towards fetishization among small press collectors. If the book is to be destroyed, does one buy two copies in order to fully "realize" one while preserving a second?

extended public performance, and one component of her larger artistic practice. The book, which is the focus of this essay, is a Risographed collection of knitting patterns and photographs based on Bebenek's close reading and translation of nine poems written by women. *k2tog*, the book, was co-published in an edition of 150 copies by Broken Dimanche Press (Berlin) and the Centre for Expanded Poetics at Concordia University (Montreal) and was designed by Zille Sophie Bostinius. The print run is split into a Canadian edition of 100 copies, and a German edition of 50 copies, though Bebenek did the Risograph printing for both editions herself. At 40 pages, it is chapbook sized, with a single signature that was folded and bound with 50 metres of twine and a pair of wooden knitting needles—that is, the twine was used to stitch the pages together, with the vast majority wrapped around the knitting needles. It is an astounding object to hold, somehow

both delicate and durable, something to handle with care but that also insists its reader genuinely consider dismantling it.

My interest in this essay is not to comprehensively unpack the complex layers of feminist thought, practice, art, and poetics that inform each layer of this project. More capable scholars than I will be able to position k2tog effectively within the entirety of its historical roots—indeed, Bebenek herself has begun this work in the book's introduction, as discussed below. There are essays to be written that perform close readings of the poems chosen; there are essays to be written about handcraft, textile art, and experimental poetics. The modest contribution of this essay is to look closely at *k2tog* the book to consider how its material form and mode of production complement and deepen the feminist work of the project. This will, I hope, support future consideration of Bebenek's larger practice.

THE PROJECT

Bebenek explained the genesis of the project—and of her move into a writing practice that increasingly embraces textile and craft—in an interview with Amanda Earl:

> Over time, I felt constrained by the purely lyric poetry I was being taught to write in school; I had ideas which couldn't be expressed entirely within language. As I began to see similarities between knitting and poetry, the twin histories of women's self-expression through both mediums, I couldn't help but weave them together. Now I work in performance, knitting, needle point techniques, sewing, bookmaking, and my crafting toolbox is always growing.

Bebenek's introduction to the book connects her project explicitly to women's domestic labour through history: "For millennia," she writes, "women have stayed home. We've performed the devalued domestic labour of cleaning, cooking, mending—of building a home." The Industrial Revolution afforded women the "luxury of leisure hours" which prompted "an explosion in the number of textiles and crafts being produced in the home." This process is intergenerational—women "passed down these skills from one generation to the next" and "built a history and a language through time." Knitting and reading, for Bebenek, invoke individual thinking and silence but also community and connection with other women in the present and throughout history.

The dual nature of the k2tog project—as a knitting project and a literary project—allows Bebenek to connect with lineages of poets *and* knitters. Indeed, the title "k2tog" is an abbreviation from the language of the knitting world for "knit two together." Bebenek writes in her introduction, "As I knitted these tapestries, found female poets who spoke to each other through time, I wove together the crafts of knitting & writing—already more closely aligned than I had realized." In the project, she knits together poems and poets, literary and craft histories of creativity, and modes of artistic production. She pairs lyric and concrete, the canon and the conceptual.

This brings to mind a discussion between Dani Spinosa and Kate Siklosi, editors and publishers at Gap Riot Press, included as an afterword of sorts to Spinosa's poetry collection *OO: Typewriter Poems* (2020). In a conversation about the feminist foundation of Spinosa's artistic practice, Siklosi emphasizes the importance of borrowing, citation, and exchange in feminist art:

> Like, women borrow. We borrow all the time. We borrow stories from each other to protect ourselves. We borrow each other's clothes. We borrow things from each other because for us it's an exchange, right? I actually think that like creative exchange—thought exchange—these things are critical. They're critical to forming a feminist

> community. Because that's how we band together. And that's how we build off of each other and create. And you know, citation is also a feminist act. You should be weaving stories of women that have done this work before you because they just haven't gotten that type of recognition before. It's about collaborating and building on those ideas together. And that creates, I think, an intellectual community. But the collaboration and sharing, there's a radical femininity about that. Like, that is femmeship. That is us doing this thing as women. It gets back to craftivism and domesticity and to you and I: as women, how we connect over the handcrafted items we make with Gap Riot Press.

In similar terms, Bebenek's book is thus both a hyper-focused micro-anthology and a feminist conceptual work of art that dwells in citation and exchange—Bebenek is citing poems of her choosing and offering exchange through her own artistic practice, but is also identifying citation and exchange that occurred in these same communities in the past. The book is built of three sets of linked poems: Elizabeth Bishop's "Sandpiper" (1962) and P.K. Page's glosa of the same, "Poor Bird" (1994); Sylvia Plath's "Blue Moles" (1960), Anne Sexton's "Sylvia's Death" (1963), and Maxine Kumin's "How It Is" (1974); and four translations (each by women) of Sappho's "Fragment 113." Eschewing any claim to primary authorship, Bebenek refers to herself as the "editor and translator" of the collection on the title page.[80]

The poems in question, however, are absent in their original linguistic forms. They exist only in Bebenek's translated

80 Anni Albers' seminal book *On Weaving* (1965) and Jen Bervin's more recent *Draft Notation* (2014) are precedents for Bebenek. Both artists used the typewriter, in Albers' formulation, to search for "new terms in the vocabulary of tactile language." Bervin calls these patterns "a kind of written score for a woven textile," connecting textile craft to broader aesthetic concerns and categories. Bervin's use of the term "score" even suggests the possibility of performance, a vital element in Bebenek's practice, to be discussed later.

form—that is, as knitting patterns. Her process for translating the poems is described in her introduction: "I wrote the patterns by mapping the stressed and unstressed syllables in the rhythm of each poetic line, and then translating those into knit and purl stitches. Each line of verse is a knitted row and each syllable, a stitch." As the linguistic content of the poems is translated into stitches, the only traces of semantic meaning are reserved in the poem titles.

THE POEMS

The chosen poems in *k2tog* are intimately related to one other, both within and between the three sets. Bebenek's selections demonstrate the 'considered relationships' that Anni Albers sees in weaving patterns, which is to say, Bebenek has knitted together a set of poetic, aesthetic, and philosophical concerns via her choice of poems. The absence of the text of the poems themselves drives the reader to seek them out, emphasizing them via absence.

Elizabeth Bishop's "Sandpiper" and P.K. Page's glosa, "Poor Bird," focus on searching in a continually changing landscape. The sandpiper in Bishop's poem encounters a world in constant flux as the waves arrive and retreat: "The world is a mist. And then the world is / minute and vast and clear." Bishop, and later Page, emphasize both the unknown and the knowable, if innumerable, details of existence. The glosa form embraced by Page is perfect for Bebenek's project, as it represents a kind of burrowing down into an existing work, of exploring the already-explored and searching again. Bishop's sandpiper is "Watching, rather, the spaces of sand between" its toes. Page explores the spaces between Bishop's lines, and Bebenek delves still deeper via her translation.

The Plath, Sexton, and Kumin poems are also intimately related to one another, and the set of poems picks up where the

Bishop and Page poems left off. Plath's "Blue Moles" describes coming upon two dead moles, leading to a consideration of how the moles move through the earth without sight, guided by their "outsize hands." They search constantly, as with Bishop's sandpiper, but rely on the tactile instead of the visible. Sexton picks up the image of the blue moles in her poem "Sylvia's Death," written after Plath's suicide. Sexton asks, "what is your death / but an old belonging / a mole that fell out / of one of your poems?" Kumin's poem, "How it is," then picks up two threads from the previous poems—the first, an elegy for a friend who has committed suicide (Sexton in this case), and the second, a striking "blue" image, this one of Sexton's blue jacket that Kumin is wearing after the poet's death.

The Sappho quartet that completes *k2tog* is structurally similar to the first two sets of poems, but introduces a further element of possibility via translation. Bebenek selects a famous Sapphic fragment—"neither for me honey nor the honey bee" as translated by Anne Carson—and works with one version adapted by H.D., two separate translations by Carson, and one version scanned in the Ancient Greek by a friend of Bebenek's. The H.D. translation is akin to the Page glosa—working with the existing fragment from Sappho, H.D. expands the poem. Anne Carson shows two paths through translating the same fragment—one relatively literal, and one more playful. The point—or rather, one point worth making—is that this interest in how translation creates possibilities—possible meanings, possible engagements, possible relationships—is animating for Bebenek. Bebenek refers to the works in *k2tog* as translations, and in her careful choice of poems to translate she underscores the dialogue between generations of artists. In the three sets of poems, Bebenek applies her attention to relationships between poems, between poets, and between women, and in *k2tog*, works to extend the thread.

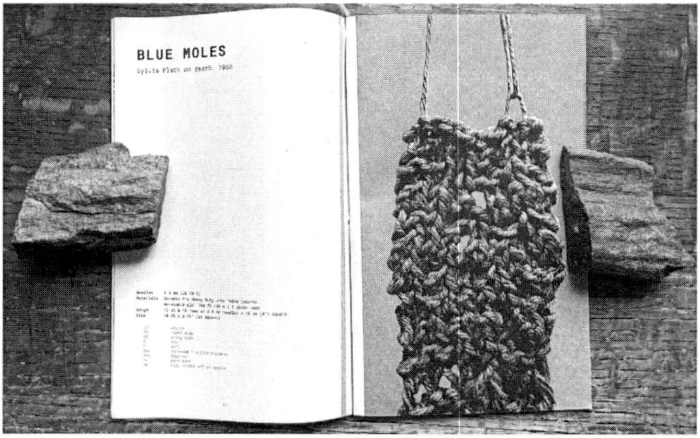

THE BOOK

k2tog is a fascinating object. Risograph-printed and twine-bound, it poses several explicit challenges to the reader. To start, the book cannot be read traditionally. Although nine poems are present, only the titles remain in meaningful semantic form. The reader—if they have the necessary knowledge of knitting patterns—could read the book and produce their own knitted poems, but even these remain one step removed from the original poems. Most readers will need to learn a new way to read—literally a new language in knitting patterns—to engage completely with the project. Bebenek insists that the poems can be "read" if one understands both languages, but what remains of the semantic content after translation is only a scansion map of stressed and unstressed syllables. That is to say, the rhythm persists, invoking the flow and silences of knitting, of thought, of reading.

In the use of scansion, Bebenek invokes a more formalist approach to literary criticism. Scansion is a dreaded cliché of the high-school and undergrad English classroom, a practice that focuses on the construction of the poem in (nearly) its smallest unit—the syllable—and can be accused at times of neglecting the content of the poem and its existence in the world. Scansion, at its least effective as a tool of literary analysis, is used to simply identify a literary text as a poem—or a particular type of poem—because it follows a particular rhythm. Bebenek flips this—scansion becomes a feminist tool to connect literary practices with another artistic mode. This connection directly informs Bostinius' design of the book.

As noted above, the book is bound using 50m of twine, the majority of which is wrapped around a pair of knitting needles attached to the spine of the book. Knitting not only informs the project conceptually, but also literally binds the project in its book form. In this, according to Bebenek via email, the book invokes "vintage knitting magazines which often came with materials needed to complete a project found in the book, a practice which continues in contemporary knitting mags." Moreover, the book is printed on lightweight earth-toned paper, something Bebenek says also emulates vintage knitting magazines. In *k2tog*, the book, the needles and twine manifest the histories Bebenek tries to contain in k2tog, the performance. This gesture insists that the reader interact with the twine and needles and presents a challenge.

As a book object, *k2tog* is awkward—it does not fit on the shelf nicely because 50m of twine are attached to it. Should the reader store the twine on top of neighbouring books on the same shelf? In behind? Should the twine be removed? Will the reader knit poems? These questions are linked to maintaining the integrity of the object—that is, leaving the twine attached—or to alternately exploring the materiality of the project—that is, knit a poem. To fit on the shelf, the book must be dismantled. To knit the poems, the reader must learn a new language, and then occupy the practices of silence, thinking, and production Bebenek explores. The "reading" available to the reader demands practice and labour, translating linguistic and semantic meanings into bodily action.[81] In

81 I confess that my copy remains intact, stored in a magazine holder alongside chapbooks.

this way, the book interrupts the order of the bookshelf, analogous to Bebenek's interruption of literary history through the project. She adapts scansion as a tool of literary analysis to fit her feminist conceptual practice. She similarly adapts the form of the book to fit the conceptual goals of her project. However the reader chooses to engage, they must confront the issue.

Broken Dimanche Press was an appropriate publisher for *k2tog* and has a history of supporting and encouraging the publication of books that push at such boundaries. In a 2013 "manifesto," the publisher declares that "The Book (qua text, literature, fiction) offers *writers* or literature a fruitful domain for experimenting with words; and the Book in turn can be treated as an exhibition space in itself." This can be seen in how the twine appears not only in the binding, but also in images reproduced within the book. Many of the poems—rather, the knitting patterns—are complemented with photographs of the finished knitted works.[82] The images capture the rough texture of the fibres of the twine in part because of the specific aesthetic qualities of the mode of printing—Risograph—a mode that further underscores the community and feminist orientations of the project, as well as its small-press investments.

Invented in Japan in the 1980s, the Risograph is a duplicator machine that looks like a photocopier on the outside, but inside houses hardware that resembles both a gestetner and a screen-printing operation. Through the use of stencils wrapped around a cylinder, the Risograph generates inexpensive, high-speed, and aesthetically interesting copies using a soy-based ink. Initially intended for something closer to business purposes, the Risograph has begun to be used by an increasing number of literary publishers—of the small and micro-varieties—for its aesthetic

82 Photographs of the knitted poems appear elsewhere, including on the cover of Heather Milne's study *Poetry Matters: Neoliberalism, Affect, and the Posthuman in Twenty-first Century North American Feminist Poetics* (University of Iowa Press, 2018).

qualities, its speed and ease and low cost per unit, as well as the enjoyment it provides the user.[83]

My own earliest experiences in publishing occurred on a Risograph. During my undergraduate years as an editor for In/Words Magazine and Press at Carleton University, our favourite mode of production (or mine anyway) was a rarely used Risograph in the photocopy room of the Department of English. In the great small-press tradition of using pilfered office supplies after hours, we would arrive after the department had closed for the day and print into the night, burning through the available stencils, cranking out chapbook after chapbook and broadside after broadside, to the rhythm of the deeply satisfying *tick* as each finished page slammed into the tray. It retained the element of the hand-made, but required less technical knowledge than letterpress printing, or a gestetner, or more complex desktop publishing software.

The use of a Risograph invokes the small press tradition of adopting business machines that have become somewhat—or extremely—outdated.[84] That the intended use for this type of machine is business related also means that it would have supported labour that was primarily coded as female—that is, copying work, administrative work—adding further dimension to its use for printing *k2tog*. Indeed, the Risograph has a fundamental connection to community work and organizing in schools, clubs, and among political activists. There is a kind of democratic access in the cost of its use. Furthermore, it is more environmentally friendly than photocopying due to its high efficiency, low-energy use, and soy-based non-toxic inks, making sustainability a fundamental element of the process.

83 A previous chapbook of Bebenek's, *Fourth Walk* (2017), was published by Toronto's now defunct Desert Pets Press (run by Catriona Wright and Emma Dolan), who consistently used risograph printing, including for Bebenek's chapbook.
84 As derek beaulieu notes in *fractal economies*, visual and concrete poetics have a history of documenting "the waste and excess produced through non-prescribed use of business machines."

Working with a Risograph is aesthetically pleasing and strikes a balance between digital and analog. Bebenek explains that the Risograph appeals partly because it is "a physically involved process, textural" that affords the printer or artist the opportunity to "play with opacities and layering." It is aesthetically pleasing partly because it pairs the promise of striving for perfection contained in the digital with the ultimate fallibility of the analog. For example, the production of colour images on Risograph is a process of repetition. Each pass through the machine prints one colour, requiring multiple passes to add layers for additional colours. To create full-colour images requires repetition, building layers and increasing the complexity of the whole. However, no two passes through the machine align perfectly. This is itself analogous to Bebenek's project. In Bebenek's words, "the riso is the perfect printing technique for *k2tog* on a metaphorical level. The Risograph prints images and words by layering individual colours and so supports the theme in the book of layering meaning, layering conversations, layering modes and iterations of creation." She groups poems that respond to each other, before herself responding. Each poem in *k2tog* is produced by a series of passes. In the imperfections of the Risograph images in the book, there is an illustration of something that the project as a whole embraces.

THE PERFORMANCES

The acknowledgements contained in the back of *k2tog* underscore the interdisciplinary nature of the project and demonstrate the discomfort—or perhaps incompleteness—of the works being consigned to the page. No literary magazines are credited; Bebenek instead thanks the various sites where the works have been presented and performed—the Gladstone Hotel (Toronto), the Centre for Expanded Poetics (Concordia, Montreal), several galleries in Toronto (White House, Gallery 345, and Dundas

Video), and the multimedia arts website *The Volta*. My first encounter with the work in person was at the Kanada Koncrete conference at the University of Ottawa in Spring 2018. Bebenek hung the knitted poems in the exhibition book fair, performed a related project throughout the conference—her knitting of the entirety of T.S. Eliot's *The Waste Land*—and also read a knitting pattern aloud at the poetry reading conducted as part of the conference.

k2tog was launched in a series of events in Montreal and Toronto that took the form of small knitting workshops.[85] The "audience" for each event dismantled their own copies in the workshop space. In this way, Bebenek manifested the connections at the heart of *k2tog*, knitting together literary and craft histories across generations. I think here of Gerard Genette's discussion of the public performance of literary work as an interpretive paratextual activity: "the reading itself, which in its delivery, its stresses, its intonations, in the gestures and facial expressions used for emphasis, is already quite obviously an 'interpretation'." *k2tog* events are interpretive on a number of levels—they interpret the form and structure of a book launch and a literary reading / performance; they interpret the poems via their translation into knitted objects; and they interpret a reader's engagement with the published book form of the project (or maybe they ask the reader to interpret their own "creative regeneration" of the book, to use McKenzie's term). Bebenek explains that she particularly enjoys "seeing all of the different iterations of the poem through knitters' styles, which is one of the main intentions of *k2tog*—to continue the chain of conversation of the original authors."

Indeed, it is perhaps in these performances, or in the efforts to encourage others to knit the poems, that Bebenek's *k2tog* finds its fullest expression. As Bebenek explained to Amanda Earl, "I'm

85 A planned presentation in Copenhagen was not possible due to the COVID-19 pandemic, but an online artist talk took its place.

inspired by how knitting patterns are a creative work by a single author which are expressly intended to be replicated, in opposition to the cult of individual genius which we find in the poetic tradition." The act of sharing the patterns, an act explicitly bound up in the history of women's crafts, positions Bebenek herself not as the central figure in this project, but rather as one node in an ongoing conversation instigated by the poems. It places the emphasis on the word *together* in the title of the project.

Since the publication of *k2tog* in 2018, Bebenek's artistic practice has increasingly embraced public performance, knitting, and fibre art, including large-scale projects such as knitting T.S. Eliot's *The Waste Land* and Ezra Pound's *The Cantos*. In *k2tog*, the book, the reader finds a print expression of a non-print performance and project and, crucially, an invitation to engage directly with the project beyond the standard definition of reading. By asking the reader to literally learn a new language and to dismantle the book in the process, the project modulates ideas of community, tradition, and participation. It is clearly both a poetry project and also something different. The openness of poet, designer, and publisher to play with the tools available to the small press accomplishes a remarkable translation of not only the poems, but also of the available forms of the book and of reading.

Uncollected: 21 Notes[86] (and 22 Footnotes[87]) on Justin Million's KEYBOARDS!

> "Poems exist to create a space for the possibilities of language as material. That is what distinguishes them from all other forms of writing. Poems allow language its inherent provisionality, uncertainty, and slippages. They also give us space for its physicality—the way it sounds, looks, feels in the mouth—to itself make meaning. And poems remind of something we almost always take for granted: the miraculous, tenuous ability of language to connect us to each other and the world around us."
>
> —Matthew Zapruder, *Why Poetry* (2017)

---

86 The "21 Notes" of this essay were originally published as the introduction to the book *EJECTA: The Uncollected KEYBOARDS! Poems* by Justin Million (Apt. 9 Press, 2020). I have left those original notes more or less intact, save some minor revisions to adjust to the new context of this book, while the footnotes are entirely new.

87 What I want to do in these footnotes is provide further context where available, expand on some of my earlier thinking in the original introduction, and think through the experience of having made a book from a project that, in its original form, was expressly and deliberately *not a book*.

KEYBOARDS! NOTE #1

In August 2016, Justin Million began what is, to date, the defining project of his life in poetry, KEYBOARDS!, a live poetry-writing performance conducted more or less monthly over the course of two years. In August 2018, Million ended the project after 30 events, some 500 poems later.[88]

KEYBOARDS! NOTE #2

KEYBOARDS! is deceptively simple in design and execution. Million would set up one of his many typewriters at The Garnet (usually)—a downtown bar in Peterborough, ON—on the last Sunday of the month around 8pm, sit down, and begin writing poems. When he completed a poem, he would ring a bell and recite the poem to the room. After he finished, the poem was placed on a barstool, available for anyone in the bar to take home.[89]

KEYBOARDS! NOTE #3

Under closer scrutiny, the project becomes more complex in its interactions with the public, with literary history, and with Million's own literary output. Imagine writing 500 poems, creating a single copy of each, performing each poem a single time, and sending that single copy out into the world (for free no less!). *EJECTA* gathers the *uncollected* poems from KEYBOARDS!—that is, 132 poems that were *not* picked up. Beyond these 132 poems, the other 368 are

88 Million offers a full account of the genesis of KEYBOARDS! in his "Typewriter Talk," an essay published in *EJECTA*.

89 The final performance in the original series of 500 poems (August 26, 2018) was filmed and is available online in an edited and condensed form under the title "KEYBOARDS Farewell."

gone. Million cannot return to them, edit them, shape them into a manuscript, send them out to magazines, or even revisit them to trace his past thinking.[90] Those (collected) poems are marked only by their absence in the numbering of the sequence.[91]

KEYBOARDS! NOTE #4

After each entirely unique performance, Million's poems acquired readerships even smaller than is normal for poetry in Canada. The ratio is one to one—one poem to one person, with each copy existing in a single library, if saved at all. The emphasis of KEYBOARDS! falls not on posterity, but on publicly performing the *act of producing the work*. KEYBOARDS! draws our attention to the fact that what happens after writing and distributing a poem is beyond the control of the poet. (Remember also that a significant portion of the typical KEYBOARDS! audience was not a literary audience, but rather simply people in a bar; some may have taken the poem home, some might have lost it on the street or on the bus, some might have written a grocery list on the back and forgotten about it altogether.)[92]

---

90 In sending the poems out into the world in this way, Million let go of the idea of a book built of the best work produced for KEYBOARDS! The book is often the thing that lends legitimacy to a poet—whatever that term means for poets these days. The book is what you can point at to say "here is proof that I am a poet" when talking to non-poets (or to other poets for that matter). And so KEYBOARDS! was to some degree an active choice to explore a poetic practice entirely separate from the idea of a book.

91 Therefore the original iteration of KEYBOARDS! exists in the 368 poems that were picked up, the intention being a kind of writing project wholly distributed with no possibility of reconstituting the whole. In this way, the 500 poems extend the irreproducibility of live readings into a printed form.

92 However, it is more than the irreproducibility of the live reading, it is that KEYBOARDS! is also emancipated from the idea of *the book*. While as a whole it has perhaps more individual readers than many books of poetry published in this country, each reader has only a small piece of a much larger project. The book object commemorating KEYBOARDS! is entirely fragmentary, wholly uncollected.

KEYBOARDS! NOTE #5

All poetry readings are elusive after the fact, not quite captured effectively by a description or a recording. KEYBOARDS! amplifies this by its suggestion of materiality. It *feels* collectable and graspable somehow, even though its final product is disparate. The project paired the smallest print run possible—a single copy—with a notably large output—500 poems in two years—and was ultimately distributed to an unknown number of individuals.

KEYBOARDS! NOTE #6

Million's sequential numbering gives the impression that the series is carefully accounted for, but this too is misleading.[93] As close readers will note, numbers repeat in the sequence. There are also poems outside of the primary 500. KEYBOARDS! existed briefly as a show on Trent Radio in Peterborough. Million would, as in standard KEYBOARDS! shows, set up his typewriter, write poems, and read them on completion. To fill the airspace as he typed, he played classical music. The radio show is archived and available to be streamed on demand, reproducing those poems (or at least rendering them reproducible). The Trent Radio poems are numbered individually outside the primary 500. There was a lost episode of the show, recorded but never broadcast or archived, and a home recording for an ill-fated attempt to perform a KEYBOARDS! "duel" against himself using two separate typewriters, something that was more successful when other poets were invited to participate (see Notes #15 and #18). KEYBOARDS! was also performed at the ReFrame Film Festival. None of these poems are represented in the primary numbered sequence of 500 poems.[94]

93 On the top right of each page, Million typed "KEYBOARDS! Poem #__."

94 KEYBOARDS! has also continued in other forms since the publication of

KEYBOARDS! NOTE #7

This type of project is, I should add, the stuff of nightmares for archivists and collectors. In that, I am an odd person to write this essay or to have published *EJECTA*—KEYBOARDS! magnifies things about small press book history that cause me distress. As a long-time friend and reader of Million, and as a collector of small press works, I wonder about the literally hundreds of poems he's written that I will never get to read, I fret about the ones already destroyed, and I quietly (optimistically) anticipate the ones that will find their way to me in some future year.[95]

KEYBOARDS! NOTE #8

KEYBOARDS! champions a radical mode of production. It is a performance in which the process of writing poetry is performed more than the poetry itself, positing the act of writing as something worthy of performance and audience. Moreover, it argues that this act exists intellectually, emotionally, and physically *in the world*. The intended audience is present for the entire process. It is not an ideal audience of readers well versed in the traditions the poet is engaged with, but an audience with no time to consider traditions at all. Each poem, to whatever degree it succeeded by whatever definition of poetry one subscribes to, had to live or die on a single performance to an audience of people who may

---

EJECTA, most recently at events in collaboration with Jeffrey Macklin of Jackson Creek Press (Peterborough) creating letterpress prints live in the bar next to Million using lines from the poems Million writes during the events. Counterintuitively, the small press at times tends towards expansion—small projects, projects with initial singularity of purpose, can spiral into larger projects, or into series of projects. And so with KEYBOARDS!, the initial idea of a simple numbered set of poems, composed sequentially through a single outlet, of course became a project with variants and offshoots and, eventually, the physical book that is *EJECTA*.

95 I am delighted to say that some KEYBOARDS! poems did make their way to me through the mail after *EJECTA* was published.

or may not have cared about poetry but happened to be in the right bar on a Sunday night in Peterborough (a town that boasts a proud and generative arts community, but one that I suspect does not have the numbers in its poetry audience to fill a bar most nights).[96]

KEYBOARDS! NOTE #9

The KEYBOARDS! poems show their process intimately.[97] Words are crossed out—*X'd* out—and new words are inserted;[98] the direction of thought can change in response to something in the bar; handwriting occasionally interjects; as each poem is numbered, the reader can see when dozens in a row have been taken (for example, 58 to 96 are absent) or when several in a row have gone uncollected; the pages are never quite straight. You can even trace the different typewriters used—documented in the notes at the back of *EJECTA*—by their variations in typeface and ribbon strength and key integrity.[99] Just as there is bravery in

96 The act of bringing poetry to a room full of a non-poets is one potential response to the repeated criticism that poetry has no audience outside of poets in the 21st century, and does not try to reach beyond its own relatively closed boundaries. Perhaps this type of print form (but importantly a *non-book* print form) of poetry can succeed at convincing a non-poet to spend a few moments considering poetry in their day-to-day life.

97 Million makes the point in his "Typewriter Talk" that typewriters are exceptionally loud machines to operate, especially in public. When I wrote above that these poems "show their process intimately," I was thinking about how the pages look, but the noise of the machine—the fact of the machine being operated in the bar—would have rendered the process intimately visible to bar patrons / audience members as well. Million's rhythm—each letter, each hesitation—would have imposed itself on the room to some degree.

98 In "Typewriter Talk," Million goes into more detail about his use of the "X" in this fashion: "I used capital X's to erase words [...] in order to make my mistakes more prominent, which adds another layer, literally and figuratively, to each poem."

99 While producing the book *EJECTA*, each poem was scanned and reproduced in facsimile, but the work of page layout posed interesting challenges given the specific characteristics of the poems and pages on which they were originally typewritten. I quickly had to abandon any dream of uniformity in page layout, or even type

reading a poem to a non-poetry room moments after it is written, I think there is, too, bravery in *EJECTA*. It is not a perfectly formed collection; the poet has had no room to edit. The book was not the goal of the project, but instead collects the uncollected ejecta of a 500-poem performance that argued for poetry as a mode of expression to be distributed freely, generously, and publicly.

KEYBOARDS! NOTE #10

KEYBOARDS! fits into the small press tradition of the gift economy but adjusts its focus. The gift economy, when theorized in relation to the small press, remains fairly internal. Books are shared between producers of books—that is, writers share works with writers, publishers with publishers. KEYBOARDS! focuses on sharing works with whomever was in the room during a given performance, and pries open the gift economy ever so slightly to welcome in potential new participants. That is not to say that small press folks don't share beyond the bounds of the small press, but KEYBOARDS! does so to a degree that is worthy of note.[100]

KEYBOARDS! NOTE #11

Million's distribution model echoes Lewis Hyde's insistence that gifts have "bonding power" (in contrast to the "detached nature of commodity exchange") which associates them "with community

size. I opted to retain all original variations, and simply reduced each page by the same percentage so as to guard the ratio of type size to page margins of the original poems, though I'm sure that this caused some degree of pain for any typographers who happened to flip through the book.

100 Here, again, I feel that the non-book character of the printed/typed poems is important. One cannot simply give away books (or even chapbooks) at this rate. Or, rather, most poets are not wealthy enough to do so. The cost here for Million was not financial—it was paid out in the poems themselves.

and with being obliged to others." Ailsa Craig, building on Hyde, argues that gift economics in small press communities demonstrate an "irrational commitment to something [that] most often yields only benefits internal to the field." That is, commitment to small press poetry and gift exchange is irrational given the overwhelming likelihood of anonymity, lack of recognition, and financial precarity.

KEYBOARDS! NOTE #12

I would argue that the conditions described above create space for the free exchange of gifts. Moreover, such irrationality can also make possible different modes of valuing art and productivity. Hans Abbing, in *Why Are Artists Poor? The Exceptional Economy of the Arts* (2002), argues, "money does not rule the gift sphere where there is no transparent profit motive [...]. Giving promotes other virtues like *sharing, generosity, selflessness, social justice, personal contact,* and *respect for non-monetary values*" (emphasis original). This, it seems to me, is an accurate description of how KEYBOARDS! distributes poetry and the types of virtues it champions as vital to sustaining an artistic community.

KEYBOARDS! NOTE #13

KEYBOARDS! is a culmination of Million's decade-and-a-half in the small press. He worked as an editor at In/Words Magazine and Press (Carleton University) for a handful of years as an undergraduate student, taking responsibility for the monthly reading series (The Reading Series), a role that introduced him to hosting and organizing events to support other poets. He was also one of the hosts of Literary Landscapes on CKCU FM, Carleton's community radio station, another live space in which he experimented with the public role of the poet. He is currently the poetry editor of bird, buried press (from publisher Elisha May Rubacha) and runs the Show and Tell Poetry Series.[101]

KEYBOARDS! NOTE #14

Million's "Typewriter Talk" began as an informal lecture given at Evans Contemporary Gallery in Peterborough, discussing writing, live writing, and writing on a typewriter. The original notes from that talk have been expanded to the essay contained in *EJECTA*. In it, Million makes the case for his deliberate use of the typewriter: "I wanted the typewriter to be an opportunity to grow as a poet, to stretch my poetics, and to interrogate the act of writing as I knew it through relying on a different medium to produce my finished work."

KEYBOARDS! NOTE #15

In an email discussing the idea that would become *EJECTA*, Million described the series as a "reciprocal and very localized event experience." Indeed, the series is inextricably bound to Peterborough. Jeff Blackman brought it to Ottawa for a one-off "duel" with jesslyn delia smith, but it received a response in some ways at odds with its intention—the chosen venue was full of poets visiting other poets and old friends, and poems were greedily collected (primarily by me, I confess). In Peterborough, some poetry and small press

101 I think that Million's history shows a process of learning the virtues of non-book forms of poetry—and moreover, *live* forms of poetry. Years of organizing and hosting readings, and time spent finding ways to make poetry work on the radio, could only have developed an appreciation for poetry outlets that do not necessarily rely on the book as the proper or final or inevitable home for a poem.

folks were regular attendees of Million's performances, but the bar was also full of people with no particular affinity for poetry. In this, KEYBOARDS! is an illustration of one of the conditions of being a poet—writing somehow in public but also in isolation.[102]

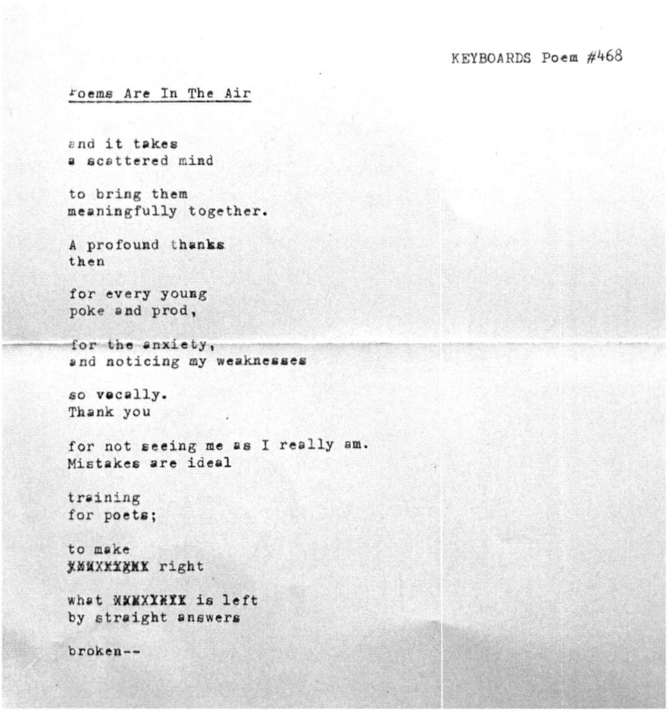

KEYBOARDS Poem #468

Poems Are In The Air

and it takes
a scattered mind

to bring them
meaningfully together.

A profound thanks
then

for every young
poke and prod,

for the anxiety,
and noticing my weaknesses

so vocally.
Thank you

for not seeing me as I really am.
Mistakes are ideal

training
for poets;

to make
XXXXXXXXX right

what XXXXXXXX is left
by straight answers

broken--

KEYBOARDS! NOTE #16

Another poet of the Peterborough–Ottawa line, Michael Dennis, spent one month sitting in a bookstore window with a typewriter (from January 7 to February 7, 1986 at the Avenue Bookshop in

102 *EJECTA* also gestured at the Peterborough origins of the project—musician, artist, and former resident Graeme Kennedy provided the cover art, while Peterborough-based photographer Andy Carroll provided two photographs taken during KEYBOARDS! events.

Ottawa), writing poems in a kind of residency, before taping them up in the window and later gathering them into one of his defining collections, *poems for jessica-flynn* (1986). Joe Blades did a similar thing in his "casemate poems" in Fredericton. rob mclennan, in 1999, repeated Dennis's act in Ottawa's legendary Octopus Books. These all strike me as different acts than KEYBOARDS!, though. These were *exceptions*, public experiments rather than sustained practices, and did not produce work to distribute without duplicate. Even in the world of small and smaller and micro-press publishing, producing 500 unique works in editions of 1 is, to my knowledge, unheard of.[103]

KEYBOARDS! NOTE #17

KEYBOARDS! can be seen alongside other live performances of writing and publishing in the contemporary small press scene—Michael e. Casteels sitting at a table at a small press book fair making books by hand for his Puddles of Sky Press, Elisha May Rubacha's live bookmaking for bird, buried press in multiple public spaces (including galleries and twice at KEYBOARDS! performances), or Jessica Bebenek's public knitting and fibre art performances as part of her wide-ranging poetic practice. These all foreground physical labour and the physical body, and insist that each should form public components of literary and artistic production.[104]

---

103 I have since remembered the "Multiple Originals" project from The Alternative Press in the 1970s, through which poets were asked to write 500 original poems on a numbered set of 500 postcards, among them Alice Notley, Robert Creeley, and Ted Berrigan.

104 In the case of Bebenek particularly, as discussed in the previous essay, the turn away from the book towards the performance is notable, including the active participation of the reader. The audience at a KEYBOARDS! show is implicated as well, albeit more passively. Whereas Bebenek asked attendees to dismantle their copies of *k2tog* and knit poems, the audience at a KEYBOARDS! show simply had to go on with their night, and might have found that something they did or said

KEYBOARDS! NOTE #18

Despite the radically restricted distribution of the majority of the KEYBOARDS! poems, there are more traditional material traces of the series. Rubacha's bird, buried press has live-published two books at KEYBOARDS! events. The first, *Beyond Repair* was published in July 2017 in an edition of 5 copies, each of which has 4 unique KEYBOARDS! poems enclosed. The second, *Dual*, was published in an edition of 20 in January 2017 at one of the two duelling KEYBOARDS! events, this one with Jeff Blackman (each copy includes one unique KEYBOARDS! poem each by Million and Blackman).

KEYBOARDS! NOTE #19

EJECTA is a kind of photographic negative of KEYBOARDS!, an event that was, in its design, resistant to precisely the kind of collecting happening in the book. We tried to counteract this contradiction by inserting the original typescripts of the "uncollected" KEYBOARDS! poems into copies of the book. This includes the 132 poems reproduced in *EJECTA* as well as 12 that are not. These 12 additional poems were written for the radio show and the ReFrame Film Festival incarnations of KEYBOARDS! respectively.[105]

---

wound up in a poem.

105 Part of the idea here was that if we succeeded in selling 144 copies of the book, all of the original KEYBOARDS! typescripts would be gone.

KEYBOARDS! NOTE #20

EJECTA does, however, try to enact something of the generosity of KEYBOARDS! in its desire to share. Within, we surrounded the uncollected poems with contextual materials to document the series but also to echo its general unwieldiness and undocumentability. In addition to the poems and this essay, the reader will find Million's "Typewriter Talk," a cast of the typewriters used,[106] and a chronology of the events.

KEYBOARDS! NOTE #21

The epigraph to these notes comes from Matthew Zapruder's book of essays, *Why Poetry*. In an interview conducted by Ben Ladouceur, Million expands on Zapruder's championing of "the miraculous, tenuous ability of language to connect us to each other and the world around us" when he describes how KEYBOARDS! engages its audience:

> [...] there is a unique dynamic inherent in mining a live audience for poetic material, and then including that audience's voice directly in the work. Folks are chuffed to be included in a poem, as most audience members have little to no experience with poetry. Some folks who attend are downright against poetry, so it's a challenge to enter their space and do your own thing. [...] it might amount to no more than a peace offering between me and the audience to show them that I am here for them.

The poem as a provisional space—that is, as an *uncertain* space—is laid bare in the structure of KEYBOARDS! As Zapruder reminds

---

106 A Smith-Corona Electra 110, a Smith-Corona XL 1000, an Olympia Werke AG Wilhelmshaven Portable, and a Smith-Corona Corona 12.

us, however, the poem is also necessarily physical, something else that KEYBOARDS! insists on reminding its audience/listener/reader in its performance on stage and in its primary material trace—the typewritten poem. Million describing the difficulty of entering the space of an audience reminds us of the difficulty of establishing the connection that Zapruder describes, but also reminds us of the value of striving to do so.[107]

107 *EJECTA* was perhaps a failure if measured against Zapruder's terms. It is precisely the kind of book that is likely to turn off a non-poet reader—it contains what may appear to be too many poems for a single book, as well as two essays and a pile of contextual notes. It did strive, however, to document an astounding poetic project that was itself fundamentally resistant to documentation. It is a large and unwieldy book that responded to a large and unwieldy project by trying to reconcile the live *and* non-book print inclinations of KEYBOARDS! with the realities of a printed book, and in that I feel it was a success.

Postscript

> "It's a space that makes a space—the book opens to vastness."
> —Jen Bervin, *The Book: 101 Definitions* (2021)

I won't pretend to be able to offer a tidy conclusion to this set of essays. I do feel, however, that there are related concerns animating each essay in this book, and as a result, some related questions are posed by the collection as a whole.

These essays are, to different degrees, anxious about preservation and loss, particularly of the underappreciated, the undocumented, and even the unnoticed in the small press. Why are some bookmakers acknowledged and celebrated, while others are consigned to obscurity? How does the small press prod at the boundaries of bookmaking, and what would our histories of the book in Canada look like if we made more room for the weirder objects that have been produced by our smaller small and micropresses? And further still, what are the stakes of documenting this work? Does it matter, fundamentally, if we can never again see this book or that book the way that it was initially published? Is there something antithetical or contradictory in documenting and discussing work that was never intended to be widely accessible? What happens to a book or broadside or leaflet when it is removed from its original setting, whether the manner in which it was printed or distributed (gift-economic or otherwise)?

I don't have answers to any of these questions, but they do seem to me to be based on ideas worth sitting with. I have tried to at least identify and articulate these questions, and others, with as much clarity as such inherently disordered subject matter allows. The small press, it seems to me, is notable for its gleeful embrace of whatever printing tools and materials are available, and for its continual search for new and appropriate (and sometimes even inappropriate) ways to give poetry a print form. In our increasingly digital environments, the print forms taken by the small press can be both anachronistic and ground breaking, and in the freedom to be one or the other—or both at the same time—the small press is particularly suited to the publication of poetry.

At the outset of this book, I struggled to offer a working definition of the small press to help the reader navigate the essays. Its resistance to definition is perhaps absolute—but rather than a bug, I think that it is finally a feature. The struggle to define the small press derives from the constant searching by those within the small press for new publishing tools and for new ways to use existing tools. The books and chapbooks and broadsides and leaflets and envelopes and single typewritten sheets discussed in these essays agitate—lovingly, knowingly—against their own constraints as made objects, as pieces of culture, as things to be sent out into the book ecosystem to be encountered by readers. And to my eyes and hands and thinking, they are achievements; they are expressive, personal, interesting, and, to embrace the entirely subjective, beautiful. So much of the most exciting bookmaking in Canada today is to be found on tables at small press book fairs, and it is work that will continue in the future regardless of the answers to any of the questions I have tried and failed to answer in the preceding pages. It will find a new form using the tools at its disposal, and a new form after that, and book culture and history in Canada will be richer for it.

Works Consulted

Abbing, Hans. *Why Are Artists So Poor? The Exceptional Economy of the Arts*. Amsterdam: Amsterdam University Press, 2002.

Albers, Annie. *On Weaving*. London: Studio Vista, 1965.

Anstee, Cameron. *I simply began: above/ground press at 20 [an interview with rob mclennan]*. Ottawa: Apt. 9 Press, 2013.

Ball, Nelson. *The Pre-Linguistic Heights*. Toronto: Coach House, 1970.

Ball, Nelson and Barbara Caruso. *Points of Attention*. Toronto: Weed/Flower Press, 1971.

beaulieu, derek. *fractal economies*. Vancouver: Talonbooks, 2006.

---. "Linguistic Fragmentation as Political Intervention in Calgarian poetics." *Open Letter* 13:6 (Summer 2008): 107-117.

beaulieu, derek and Jason Christie. "Six Notes Towards a Poetics of The Small Press." *Open Letter* 12.4 (Fall 2004): 7-10.

beaulieu, derek and rob mclennan. *Economies of Scale: rob mclennan interviews derek beaulieu on NO PRESS / derek beaulieu interview rob mclennan on above/ground press*. Ottawa: above/ground press, 2012.

Bebenek, Jessica. Email to the author. December 31, 2020.

---. *k2tog*. Montreal / Berlin: Centre for Expanded Poetics / Broken Dimanche Press, 2018.

Beckman, Joshua. *Three Talks*. Seattle and New York: Wave Books, 2018.

Bencke, Ida and John Holden. "Manifesto: 2013 Year of The BDP Avant Garde." *Publishing Manifestos: an international anthology from artists and writers.* Edited by Michalis Pichler. Cambridge: MIT Press, 2019. 222-223.

Benjamin, Water. "The Work of Art in the Age of Mechanical Reproduction." *Illuminations: Essays and Reflections.* Ed. Hannah Arendt. New York: Schocken Books, 1985. 217-251.

---. "Unpacking My Library: A Talk about Book Collecting." *Illuminations: Essays and Reflections.* Ed. Hannah Arendt. New York: Schocken Books, 1985. 59-67.

Bergin, Jenny. "Technical Competence of Fran Jones superb." *Ottawa Citizen.* 21 April 1969. 12.

Bervin, Jen. "Draft Notation." *Jen Bervin.* n.d. Web.

Birney, Earle. "Poets and Painters: Rivals or Partners?" *Canadian Art* 14.4 (Summer 1957): 148-150.

Bishop, Elizabeth. "Sandpiper." *Poems.* Edited by Saskia Hamilton. New York: Farrar, Straus, and Giroux, 2011. 129.

Bowering, George. "Poets in their Twenties." *Canadian Literature* 20 (Spring 1964): 54-64.

---. "Purdy: Man and Poet." *Canadian Literature* 43 (Winter 1970): 24-35.

Brahms, Flemming. "Interview." *Kunapipi* 2.2 (1980): 117-127.

Bringhurst, Robert. *The Elements of Typographic Style: Version 3.2.* Vancouver: Hartley & Marks, 2008.

---. *The Surface of Meaning: Books and Book Design in Canada* Burnaby: Canadian Institute for Studies in Publishing, 2008.

Butling, Pauline and Susan Rudy. *Writing in Our Time: Canada's Radical Poetries in English (1957–2003).* Waterloo: Wilfred Laurier University Press, 2005.

Camlot, Jason and J.A. Weingarten, eds. *Unpacking the Personal Library: The Public and Private Life of Books.* Waterloo: Wilfrid Laurier University Press, 2022.

Campbell, Wanda. "Strange Plantings: Robert Kroetsch's *Seed Catalogue.*" *Studies in Canadian Literature* 21.1 (1996): 17-36.

Canadian Author and Bookman 38.4 (Summer 1963).

Carson, Anne. "146." *If Not, Winter: Fragments of Sappho*. New York: Vintage Books, 2003. 295, 379.
Carter, Alex. "Show and Sell." *Ottawa Journal*. 20 April 1974. 35.
Caruso, Barbara. *!*. Paris, ON: presspresspress, 1989.
---. *And*. Paris, ON: presspresspress, 1989.
---. "AN&D." *Impulse* 16.1 (1990): 14.
---. "Autobiography." *Open Letter*. Sixth Series, Number 1 (1986): 11-14.
---. *Citing Light*. Paris, ON: presspresspress, 1990.
---. "The Colour Lock Paintings 1969–1983." *Wording the Silent Art*. Toronto: The Mercury Press, 2001. 120-159.
---. "earth song." *The Cosmic Chef: An Evening of Concrete*. Ed. bpNichol. Ottawa: Oberon Press, 1970. 33.
---. "Foreword." Seripress Fonds. McMaster University, 1987.
---. *In Nature In Painting*. Paris, ON: presspresspress, 1988.
---. Letter to jwcurry. 8 November 1988.
---. "THE MOST DIFFICULT..." *The Cosmic Chef: An Evening of Concrete*. Ed. bpNichol. Ottawa: Oberon Press, 1970. 6.
---. *A Painter's Journey: 1966–1973*. Toronto: The Mercury Press, 2005.
---. *A Painter's Journey Volume II: 1974–1979*. Toronto: The Mercury Press, 2008.
---. *A Play for Henry Moore*. Paris, ON: presspresspress, 1989.
---. *Philosophy*. Paris, ON: presspresspress, 1990.
---. "The Seripress Collaborations: Nichol & Caruso." *St. Art: The Visual Poetry of bpNichol*. Ed. Gil McElroy. Charlottetown, PEI: Confederation Centre Art Gallery and Museum, 2000. 47-60.
---. *Silence*. Paris, ON: presspresspress, 1990.
---. *Silence*. Ottawa: Room 302 Books, 2018.
---. *Sky*. Paris, ON: presspresspress, 1990.
---. "Small Paintings." *Wording the Silent Art*. Toronto: Mercury Press, 2011. 160.
---. "Telling About Line Telling." *Wording the Silent Art*. Toronto: Mercury Press, 2011. 110-113.
Caruso, Barbara and bpNichol. *The Adventures of Milt the Morph in Colour*. Toronto: Seripress, 1972.

---. *H: An Excursion*. Toronto: Seripress, 1976.
Christopher's Movie Matinee. Dir. Mort Ransen. National Film Board, 1968. Film.
Clay, Steve and M.C. Kinniburgh. *After Words: Visual and Experimental Poetry in Little Magazines and Small Press 1960–2025*. New York City: Granary Books, 2025.
Cockburn, Bruce. Preface. *Dancing Alone: Selected Poems*. By William Hawkins. Fredericton: Broken Jaw Press (cauldron books 5), 2005. 9.
"Contributors Page." *Evidence* 6 (n.d.): 119.
Cooley, Dennis. *The Home Place*. Edmonton: University of Alberta Press, 2016.
---. "On Robert Kroetsch and Turnstone." *Prairie Fire* 37.4 (Winter 2016/2017): 86-88.
Craig, Ailsa. "Sustainability, Reciprocity, and the Shared Good(s) of Poetry." *The Journal of Arts Management, Law, and Society* 37.3 (2007): 257-270.
curry, jw. *1cent* #271. Toronto: 1cent, 1991.
---. "Cold Mountain." *Flickr*. 28 October 2015. Web.
---. *MORF MY WINDOW*. Ottawa: TesserActual ArteFactory, 2016.
Dalgleish, Melissa. "Her Constellated Mind: Jay Macpherson's Modernism and the Mythopoeic Turn." Dissertation, York University, 2016.
Davey, Frank. *Weeds*. Toronto: Coach House Press, 1970.
Dean, Michael and jwcurry, eds. *Headz & He&z*. Toronto: Underwhich Editions, 1985.
Drucker, Johanna. "The Self-Conscious Codex: Artists' Books and Electronic Media." *SubStance* 26.1 (1997): 93-112.
Drumbolis, Nicky. *Zomboidgibber / First Fair Letters of a User*. Toronto: Letters, 1991.
Earl, Amanda. "Interview: The Thread Between Craft and Language." *Judith: Women Making Visual Poetry*. Sweden: Timglaset Editions, 2021. 23243.

Emerson, Lori. *Reading Writing Interfaces: From the Digital to the Bookbound*. Minneapolis: University of Minnesota Press, 2014.

Fine Printing: The Private Press in Canada. Toronto: University of Toronto Press, 1995.

Fritsch, Eva. Email to the author. March 25, 2017.

Geddes, Gary. *15 Canadian Poets x3*. Toronto: Oxford University Press, 2001.

Genette, Gerard. *Paratexts: Thresholds of Interpretation*. New York: Cambridge University Press, 1997.

Gewurtz, Michelle. "Ottawa Under Pressure." *We'll All Become Stories: A Survey of Art in the Ottawa-Gatineau Region*. Eds. Rebecca Basciano, Jim Burant, Michelle Gewurtz, Catherine Sinclair. Ottawa / Vancouver / Berkeley / London: Ottawa Art Gallery / Figure 1, 2017. 165-174.

Gillespie, Shirley. "News and Notions." *Ottawa Journal*. 14 October 1959. 32.

Gnarowski, Michael. *Contact Press 1952–1967: A Note on Its Origins and a Check List of Titles*. Montreal: Delta Canada, 1971.

Hawkins, William. Email to the author. January 31, 2012.

---. *Hawkins: 1963–1966*. Ottawa: Nil Press, 1966.

---. "King Kong Goes to Rotterdam." Ottawa: Nil Press, n.d.

---. *Ottawa Poems*. Kitchener: Weed/Flower Press, 1966.

---. "Postage Stamps." Ottawa: Nil Press, n.d.

---. "Postage Stamps." *Delta* 18 (June 1962): 9.

---. "Rubber Boots: Canto 1." Ottawa: Nil Press, n.d.

---. "A Song of Flowers." Ottawa: Nil Press, n.d.

---. "Still Life." Ottawa: Anthos Publications, 1980.

---. "Sunrise: Villanelle." Ottawa: S.A.W. Publications, n.d.

---. "Two Short Ones." Ottawa: Nil Press, n.d.

---. "Zaap." Ottawa: Nil Press, n.d.

H.D. "Fragment 113." *Selected Poems*. New York: New Directions, 1988. 447.

Hertz, Kenneth. *The Cracked Cellar*. Vancouver: Aleph House, 1990.

Hilder, Jamie. *Designed Words for a Designed World: The International Concrete Poetry Movement, 1955–1971*. Montreal and Kingston: McGill-Queens University Press, 2016.

Hyde, Lewis. *The Gift: Imagination and the Erotic Life of Property*. New York: Random House, 1983.

"Jaycees honour young men's achievements." *Ottawa Citizen*. 24 November 1966. A3.

Johnstone, Jim. *Write, Print, Fold and Staple: On Poetry and Micropress in Canada*. Kentville: Gaspereau Press, 2023.

Jones, Daniel. "Endnotes: Towards a Theory of Small Press." *Paragraph: The Fiction Magazine* 13.3 (1992): 21-24.

Ketchum, W.Q. "Robert Rosewarne." *Ottawa Journal*. 10 July 1965. 2.

Kotin, David B. and Marilyn Rueter. *Reader, Lover of Books, Lover of Heaven*. Willowdale, Ontario: North York Public Library, 1978.

Kroetsch, Robert. *Completed Field Notes: The Long Poems of Robert Kroetsch*. Toronto: McClelland and Stewart, 1989.

---. *Completed Field Notes: The Long Poems of Robert Kroetsch*. Edmonton: University of Alberta Press, 2000.

---. *The* Crow *Journals*. Edmonton: NeWest, 1980.

---. *Field Notes: The Collected Poetry of Robert Kroetsch*. Don Mills ON: General Publishing Co. Limited, 1981.

---. "For Play and Entrance: The Contemporary Canadian Long Poem." *Open Letter* 5.4 (Spring 1983): 91-110.

---. "On Being an Alberta Writer." *Open Letter* 5.4 (Spring 1983): 69-80.

---. *Seed Catalogue*. Winnipeg: Turnstone Press, 1977.

---. *Seed Catalogue*. Winnipeg: Turnstone Press, 1979.

---. *Seed Catalogue*. Winnipeg: Turnstone Press, 1986.

---. *Seed Catalogue*. Calgary: Red Deer Press, 2004.

Kumin, Maxine. "How It Is." *Poetry Foundation*. n.d. Web.

"Kwikprint Model 25 Foil Stamping Machine." *Kwikprint*. n.d. Web.

Ladouceur, Ben. "An Interview with Justin Million, host/star of KEYBOARDS!" *Open Book*. 16 March 2018. Web.

MacSkimming, Roy. Email to the author. May 31, 2018.

---. Email to the author. June 13, 2018.

---. Email to the author. January 10, 2019.

---. "William Hawkins: A Unique Voice in Canadian Poetry." *Dancing Alone: Selected Poems*. By William Hawkins. Fredericton: Broken Jaw Press (Cauldron books 5), 2005. 11-18.

Marlatt, Daphne. *Intertidal: The Collected Earlier Poems 1968–2008*. Vancouver: Talonbooks, 2017.

Martin, Colin. "At the Margins: Chapbook Presses in Canada." Dissertation, University of Calgary, 2016.

Mayne, Seymour. "Impression (For Leonard Cohen." *Delta* 22 (October 1963): Rear cover.

McCaffery, Steve. *Carnival: the first panel: 1967–70*. Toronto: Coach House Press, 1973.

McElroy, Gil. "Ground States: The Visual Contexts of bpNichol." *Gravity and Grace: Selected Writings on Contemporary Canadian Art*. Wolfville, NS: Gaspereau Press, 2001. 83-98.

McKenzie, D.F. *Bibliography and the Sociology of Texts*. Cambridge: Cambridge University Press, 1999.

McKnight, David. *Experiment: Printing the Canadian Imagination*. Edmonton: University of Alberta, 2018.

---. "Small Press Publishing." *History of the Book in Canada: Volume Three: 1918–1980*. Eds. Carole Gerson and Jacques Michon. Toronto: University of Toronto Press, 2007. 308-318.

mclennan, rob and Christine McNair. *above/ground press 20th anniversary fetish object featuring a selection of "poem" broadsides from 1999–2013 as well as a bibliography of poem broadsides published by the press from 1995–2015*. Ottawa: above/ground press, [2013].

---. *above/ground 25*. Ottawa: above/ground press, [2018].

McNair, Christine. *Charm*. Toronto: Book*hug, 2017.

---. "Poetic Conservation." *Toronto International Festival of Authors*, 10 October 2013. Web.

Miller, George L and Elizabeth A. Jorgensen. *Some Notes on Bottle Mould Numbers from the Dominion Glass Company and its Predecessors*. Ottawa: Parks Canada, 1986.

Million, Justin. Email to the author. August 13, 2018.

---. "Typewriter Talk." *EJECTA: The Uncollected KEYBOARDS! Poems*. Ottawa: Apt. 9 Press, 2020. 153-165.

Moss, Julia. "The Particulars of Space: Looking at Robert Kroetsch's *The Ledger*." *Textual Studies in Canada* 10/11 (Winter 1998): 43-54.

Nichol, bp. *Cold Mountain*. Toronto: Ganglia Press, 1966.

---. Editor. *The Cosmic Chef Glee & Perloo Memorial Society Under the Direction of Captain Poetry Presents: An Evening of Concrete*. Ottawa: Oberon Press, 1970.

---. *bpNichol Comics*. Edited by Carl Peters. Vancouver: Talonbooks, 2002.

---. "In Place: An Appreciation." *Essays on Canadian Writing* 49 (Summer 1993): 27-32.

North, Scott. "Creative Canadians: Fifth in a Series." *Ottawa Journal*. 22 October 1960. 34.

Northern Comfort. Ottawa: Commoners' Press, 1970.

Nowlan, Alden A. *Wind in a Rocky Country*. Toronto: Emblem Books, 1960.

Olson, Charles. "PROJECTIVE VERSE." *The New American Poetry*. Edited by Donald M. Allen. New York: Grove Press, 1960.

Ondaatje, Michael, ed. *The Long Poem Anthology*. Toronto: Coach House Press, 1979.

Open Letter. Sixth Series, Number 1 (1986).

Page, P.K. "Poor Bird." *Planet Earth: Poems Selected and New*. Erin, ON: The Porcupine's Quill, 2002. 63-64.

Plath, Sylvia. "Blue Moles." *The Colossus*. London: Faber and Faber, 1972. 49-50.

"Poster Poems." *Alphabet* 5 (December 1962): 9.

Purdy, Alfred. *The Blur in Between*. Toronto: Emblem Books, 1962.

Rackham, Michele. "Between the Lines: Interartistic Modernism in Canada, 1930–1960." Dissertation, McGill University, 2011.

Reaney, James. "C P R (Canadian Poetry Railroad)." *Alphabet* 4 (June 1962): 71-74.

Ricou, Laurie. Review of *Seed Catalogue* by Robert Kroetsch. *Arts Manitoba* 1.3/4 (1978), 114-115.

Ridley, Sandra. "On the Handmade (Part 2): Q&A with Christine McNair." *Open Book*, 8 September 2014. Web.

Rosewarne, Robert V. "Canadian Base Numbers." *Glasfax* 5.4 (1971): 25-56.

---. Letter to Kenneth Hertz. October 23, 1963. Kenneth V. Hertz Fonds, Library and Archives Canada.

Sarah, Robyn. "Waiting for the Operation." *Michigan Quarterly Review* 37.3 (Summer 1998). Web.

"Seripress Collection." *The University Library Special Collections*. The University of Sheffield, n.d. Web.

Sexton, Anne. "Sylvia's Death." *Poetry Foundation*. n.d. Web.

Shearer, Karis. "The Poet-Editor and the Small Press: Michael Ondaatje and *The Long Poem Anthology*." *Anthologizing Canadian Literature: Theoretical and Cultural Perspectives*. Edited by Robert Lecker. Waterloo: Wilfrid Laurier University Press, 2015. 219-252.

Shoesmith, John. *A Death Greatly Exaggerated: Canada's Thriving Small and Fine Press*. Toronto: Thomas Fisher Rare Book Library, University of Toronto, 2013.

Siklosi, Kate and Dani Spinosa. "'Like, That is Femmeship': An afterword in feminist conversation between Dani Spinosa and Kate Siklosi." *OO: Typewriter Poems*. Picton: Invisible Publishing, 2020. 67-75.

Sons of Captain Poetry. Dir. Michael Ondaatje. 1970. Film.

Speller, Randall. "Frank Newfeld and McClelland & Stewart's Design for Poetry Series." *The Devil's Artisan: A Journal of the Printing Arts* 56 (Spring/Summer 2005): 3-36.

Tostevin, Lola Lemire. "Barbara Caruso: New Configurations for an Old Alphabet." *Open Letter* Eleventh Series, Number 7 (Spring 2003): 5-15.

Toye, William. *The Oxford Companion to Canadian Literature*. Toronto: Oxford University Press, 1983.

Tratt, Grace. *Check List of Canadian Small Presses: English Language*. Halifax: Dalhousie University Library, 1974.

Tschichold, Jan. "Clay in a Potter's Hand." *The Form of the Book: Essays on the Morality of Good Design*. Vancouver: Hartley & Marks, 1991. 3-7.

---. "Graphic Arts and Book Design." *The Form of the Book: Essays on the Morality of Good Design*. Vancouver: Hartley & Marks, 1991. 8-11.

Van Herk, Aritha. "Ardently Archiving." *Topia: Canadian Journal of Cultural Studies* 20 (2008): 155-166.

Wah, Fred. "Introduction." *Completed Field Notes: The Long Poems of Robert Kroetsch*. By Robert Kroetsch. Edmonton: University of Alberta Press, 2000. ix-xvi.

---. *Scree: The Collected Earlier Poems, 1962–1991*. Vancouver: Talonbooks, 2015.

Webb, Phyllis. *Peacock Blue: The Collected Poems*. Vancouver: Talonbooks, 2014.

Weiselberger, Carl. "Of Dadaism, Nietzsche and Zen Buddhism." *Ottawa Citizen*. 20 February 1962. 17.

Wells, Christopher. Email to the author. May 28, 2018.

---. Email to the author. May 29, 2018.

---. Email to the author. May 30, 2018.

Woodcock, George. *Canadian Poets 1960–1973: A Checklist*. Toronto: Dundurn, 1976.

Zapruder, Matthew. *Why Poetry*. New York: Ecco, 2017.

Notes and Acknowledgements

Works from the Blue R Hand Press, Emblem Books, and Nil Press are reproduced with the respective permissions of the Estate of Andries Hamann, the Estate of William Hawkins, the Estate of Jay Macpherson, the Estate of Alden Nowlan, the Estate of Al Purdy, the Estate of Robert Rosewarne, and the Estate of Chris Wells. Works from Seripress and presspresspress are reproduced with the respective permissions of the Estate of Barbara Caruso and the Estate of bpNichol. Works from Turnstone Press are reproduced with the respective permissions of Turnstone Press, Eva Fritsch, and the Estate of Robert Kroetsch. Works from above/ground press are reproduced with the respective permissions of above/ground press, Sharon Harris, rob mclennan, Christine McNair, and Sandra Ridley. Works from Broken Dimanche Press are reproduced with the respective permissions of Broken Dimanche Press and Jessica Bebenek. Works from Justin Million and Apt. 9 Press are reproduced with the respective permissions of Justin Million and Apt. 9 Press. Thank you to each, and to Peter Bowie, Sharon Caseburg, Smaro Kamboureli, Leslie Miller, Eleanor Nichol, John

Nowlan, Jamis Paulson, Peter Reiner, Laurie Rosewarne, Stuart Ross, Laurie Siblock, Carolyn Wells, Howard White, and Chelsey Young. My efforts to contact the Estate of Fran Jones were unsuccessful.

The following essays were previously published, sometimes in different forms:

"Ottawa / you know nothing / of poems: Fran Jones, Robert Rosewarne, and the Small Press in 1960s Ottawa" in *The Devil's Artisan: A Journal of the Printing Arts* 85 (Fall/ Winter 2019).

"Incomplete Field Notes: Eva Fritsch, Turnstone Press, and the Print Histories of Robert Kroetsch's 'Seed Catalogue' and *Seed Catalogue* (1977)" in *Robert Kroetsch: Essayist, Novelist, Poet* (Ottawa: University of Ottawa Press, 2020) edited by David Staines. Reproduced with permission of the University of Ottawa.

"Uncollected: 21 Notes (and 22 Footnotes) on Justin Million's KEYBOARDS! (2016–2018)" in *EJECTA: The Uncollected KEYBOARDS! Poems* (Ottawa: Apt. 9 Press, 2020) by Justin Million.

Drafts have also been presented at the Canadian Literature Symposium (University of Ottawa) and at ACCUTE/Congress. Thank you to the editors, publishers, conference organizers, panel chairs, and my fellow panelists for supporting this work. Thank you to the subjects of these essays (and their friends and families) for your openness and generosity in discussing your work with me. Thank you to friends for conversations about these and other ideas that made possible the work contained in these essays. In addition to the names listed above, an incomplete list of these people includes Nelson Ball, Barbara Caruso, Dennis Cooley, jwcurry, Phil Hall, William Hawkins, Tim Inkster, Roy MacSkimming, Don McLeod, Alexander Monker, Tim Orlik, David Staines, Robert Stacey, Collett Tracey (1963-2026) and the In/Words team (immediate and extended), and Christopher Wells.

Thank you to Aimee Parent Dunn, Jim Johnstone, Ellie Hastings, and all at Palimpsest Press.

This book, like many things in my life, owes a debt to my father, Rod Anstee. His ongoing research into local history is responsible for some of the primary research upon which the first essay is built, and his influence on me as a reader and book collector informs the others as well as my own life in books.

Thank you, finally, to my partner Jenn for always listening patiently when I get going about this stuff, for building a life with me that makes so much room for so many books and ideas about books, for the photograph on the cover of this book, and for your design eye and help stitching chapbooks over the years. My thanks also to Beans, Mae, Harrie, and June for more or less respecting the house rule not to chew on books.

PHOTO CREDIT: JENNIFER HUZERA

Cameron Anstee is the author of two books of poetry, *Sheets: Typewriter Works* (Invisible Publishing, 2022) and *Book of Annotations* (Invisible Publishing, 2018), and the editor of *The Collected Poems of William Hawkins* (Chaudiere Books, 2015). He is the editor and publisher of Apt. 9 Press and holds a Ph.D. in English Literature from the University of Ottawa. He posts photos of small press books in his collection on Instagram (@smallpress_bookshelf).

This book was set in Dair.

The Dair typeface is a restoration—by Nick Shinn—of the Cartier typeface, which was designed by Carl Dair in 1967. Cartier was the first Canadian-designed Roman typeface (set for print/text).